the bad one

A MEMOIR ABOUT
GROWING UP A GOAT

ERIN TYLER

Copyright © 2020 Erin Tyler.

The Bad One
A Memoir About Growing Up a Goat

All rights reserved. This book or any portion thereof may not be reproduced or used in any manner whatsoever without the express written permission of the publisher except for the use of brief quotations in a book review.

Printed in the United States of America.

First printing, 2020.

HARDCOVER ISBN: 978-1-5445-0532-9
PAPERBACK ISBN: 978-1-5445-0828-3

LIONCREST PUBLISHING | AUSTIN, TEXAS
WWW.LIONCREST.COM

For Murph.

And for all the goats.

scape·goat

/ˈskāpˌgōt/

noun

(In the Bible) A goat sent into the wilderness after the Jewish chief priest had symbolically laid the sins of the people upon it *(Lev. 16)*...

scape·goat

/ˈskāpˌgōt/

noun

...A person who is blamed for the wrongdoings, mistakes, or faults of others.

THE BAD ONE
PART ONE

WRITING

ERIN LEIGH TYLER

VOTED

most likely to

FALL THE FUCK APART

— NEXT YEAR —

JAMESTOWN HIGH SCHOOL · CLASS OF 1995

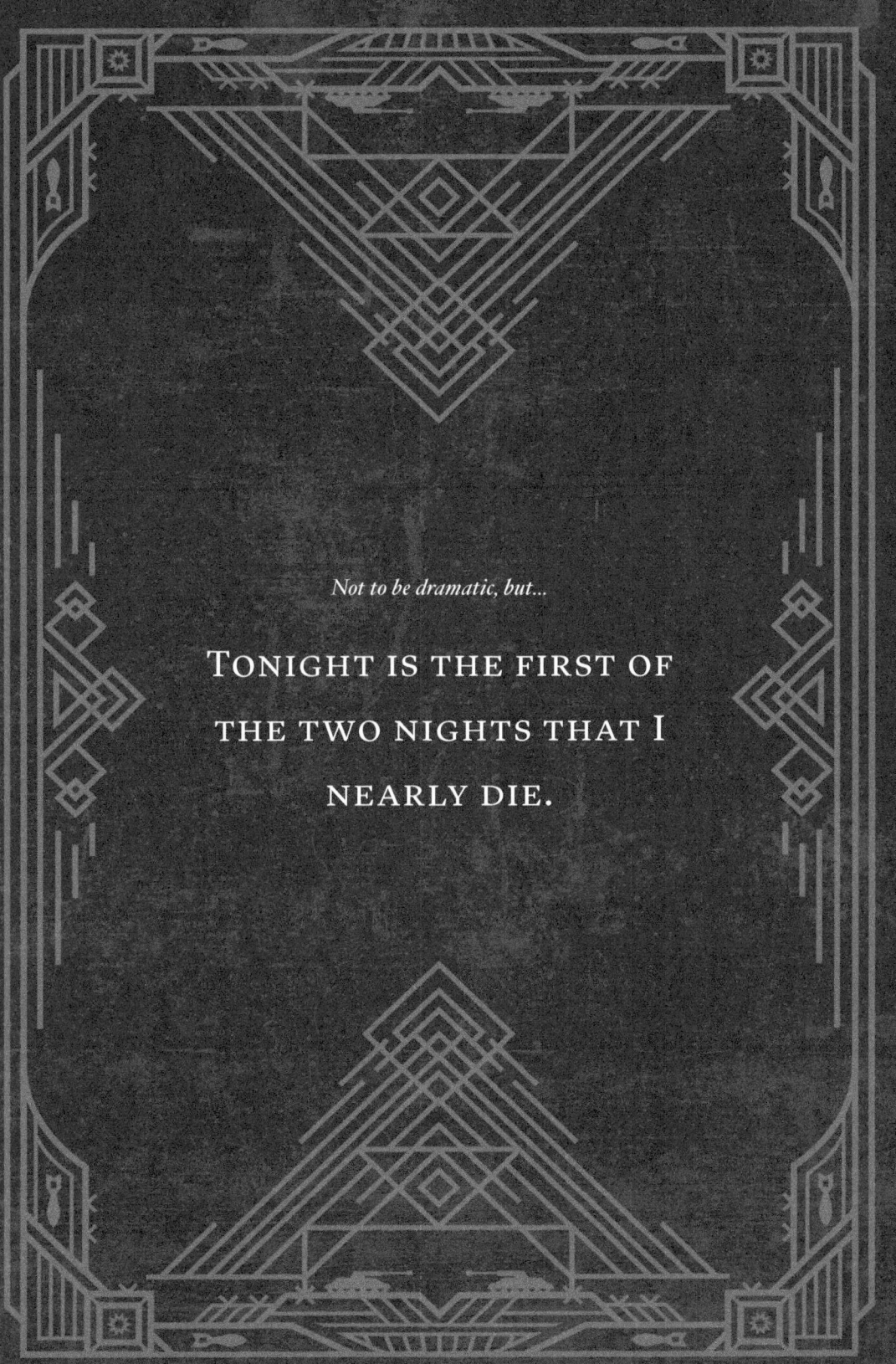

Not to be dramatic, but...

TONIGHT IS THE FIRST OF THE TWO NIGHTS THAT I NEARLY DIE.

THE GOAT WALKS OFF

Rochester, New York — 1997

A nerdy boy hands me a bottle of something called Rumple Minze. It tastes like cold mouthwash, and it makes my insides warm. I don't like the taste of it, but I like the way it makes me feel.

I have always liked the way alcohol makes me feel, because it makes me feel like I don't have to be me.

The bottle moves around the circle of people I'm standing in, and I watch as they take sips, too, and grimace. They giggle at each other and egg each other on. I watch the bottle as it jiggles in the grip of the tall, thin boy who invited us to the party, panic rising in my stomach as the seconds tick by. He's taking too long with the bottle, looking at it, checking the percentage of alcohol by volume, making a big deal about the number. The seconds tick. He hands the bottle to the next boy, who drinks and makes the same dramatic face.

I fear the spell will wear off, and I'll be dragged back into myself. That would be *intolerable.*

The boy holds the neck of the bottle, gesticulating as he launches into a story about some stupid band. The Rumple Minze sloshes around, and seconds tick.

Come on, COME ON!

I walk across the circle and grab the bottle; I tip it up and pour far too much into my mouth. Two whole swallows. I hear a noise of collective surprise from the circle, and one "whoa." Nobody is giggling anymore.

I give the bottle back and smile, nervously. Is it happening, already? Have these people already figured out I am broken?

THERE'S NO HIDING FROM THEM, ERIN. THEY WILL KNOW YOU ARE WORTHLESS.

I have won a scholarship to be here. I don't know that I could afford to be here, otherwise. I make art that could probably be called good—controlled, well-crafted graphics that aren't earth-shatteringly outstanding, like they should be if my parents are ever going to love me. The panel of judges at the scholarship competition called them technically decent and somewhat void of feeling.

I don't want to tell these people I'm a design student. People at this school think art is a waste of time, probably. I don't know. Everyone thinks real jobs require science and math.

That's what Mom and Dad think. My older sister, Marnie, went to Syracuse to study communications, which is a more sensible and marketable degree, and this is just one of the many reasons she is better than me.

My parents had driven me to school a few weeks prior. Mom had packed all my things in green plastic bins she bought at the Jamesway. She was very excited about the plastic bins. She liked storage containers a lot, and she didn't want me packing my own things because I wouldn't do it correctly.

I didn't unpack things correctly, either, so Mom took over. I sat on my dorm room bed and tried to not feel the wrong things. I hung up some inspirational running posters on the walls while mom set up my dresser drawers—pajamas at the bottom, then active wear, then tops and pants, and finally socks and underwear. That was how she liked my dressers to be. Mom pulled out my panties and began folding them the way she liked to fold them, and this made me feel incredibly angry for a reason I didn't understand. She flipped them this way and that, in front of my father, and in front of my new roommate and her mother, who seemed to find it bizarre. My insides burned with embarrassment.

If I were a good daughter, I would just let her do whatever she wanted, and I wanted to be a good daughter. Problem was, I felt the wrong things all the time.

When mom unfolded a pre-folded period panty and inspected the crotch for stains as my new roommate and her mother looked on in stunned silence, I couldn't take it anymore.

"Mom, stop!" I said, hot in the face and sweaty from anger.

Her face became frightening in an old, familiar way—with the bulging eyes, about to pop as if something behind them was expanding at a dangerous rate. It was a face that made me shit myself with fear.

She grabbed the pile of panties on my dresser and threw them at me. She called me a bitch and began to sob, running from the room. The panties fell to the floor in a little silken pile of disgrace and I felt ashamed of myself.

"Look what you did," said my father, running after her.

"Sorry," I said to my new roommate. "Sorry," I said to my roommate's mother.

YOU'RE THE WORST DAUGHTER EVER, ERIN. THEY JUST MET YOU AND THEY ALREADY KNOW IT.

The blond boy with the curls and the green jacket wants to talk to me. We sit down next to each other on a gross green couch with stains on it.

"What's up?" I ask.

"I like your sweater," he says.

"Oh," I say.

"Do you want a drink?" he asks.

"Yes," I say, quietly. *Yes. Yes! Please god, yes.*

He scoops a red cup into a cooler full of sweet punch and fruit. He hands me the cup and, though I am already very drunk, I take big gulps of it. I cannot feel like me tonight.

I have done little more than run and vomit in the first few weeks I've been here. I go to class, go for runs, eat plate after plate of food in the cafeteria, and vomit it back up in the library bathroom. As far as new independent life launching goes, this is an objectively terrible start.

He asks me what my major is and I don't want to tell him.

REAL JOBS ARE SCIENCE AND MATH JOBS.

"I am studying graphic design," I say, trying to sound smart.

"Oh" he says, feigning interest. He doesn't care.

He puts his arm around my shoulder, and it is heavy and uncomfortable. His name is Adrian, he tells me, and if there is anything I want, he can get it for me.

I want another drink. I want more Rumple Minze. I want to be perfect so I will be loved. I want to be the best, so I am worthy of it. I want to be everything I am not.

I stand up and nearly fall over. My legs are as wobbly as a

newborn goat's.

I stumble back to the circle and search out the Rumple Minze bottle. I need more, and I don't care what they think about it any more. *Fuck them. Fuck everyone.*

This is my last memory of the Rumple Minze party.

THE
SPACESHIP

A GALAXY SOMEWHERE
FAR, FAR INSIDE...

I think I must be dreaming, but maybe I am not. I hear people saying things to me, but I cannot answer them. My mouth won't work. I think I should just lie here because I am dreaming.

I feel a pain in my nose and in my throat, as if someone has threaded a big scratchy rope up my nose and out of my mouth, and yanked it back and forth. My eyes are too heavy to lift and my arms will not move. I try to wiggle a toe.

"Erin!" says someone close to my ear. There is a clapping sound. It takes all my internal energy to muster an inquisitive moaning noise.

"Erin!" I hear. "Stay with us."

I drift off.

What dream is this? I wonder.

Or is this real? It seems so real.

There are white lights above me, flashing and moving. I am inside a futuristic tube. I briefly entertain the idea that I have been abducted by aliens, recalling that movie from the nineties about the lumberjack from Arizona who was scooped up in a beam of light and poked in the eye with an alien probe. I had nightmares for months about that.

My left eye will not open. It is throbbing for some reason I cannot understand. I curl my toes and stretch my body out, take a deep breath in and notice a terrible odor somewhere nearby. Someone has vomited, a lot—an offensive amount—and the vomit has been cooking for a time, like hot gutter vomit during street festivals.

I pick my head up and look down at my body. My sweater and jeans are covered in sticks, dirt, and a slime-like substance that looks an awful lot like vomit. My neck is awful stiff and sore.

"Hold still!" says a voice outside the alien tube.

"What?" I say. *Where the fuck am I?*

"You're in a CAT scan!"

Aw, shit.

⏪

The day I found out I had won my scholarship to RIT was the best day of my life.

A letter came in the mail addressed to me from the university, and Mom had opened it for me. Dad met me in the kitchen as I came home from a run, beaming with pride and waving the letter in my face. "You won!" he said. "You beat them all!" He gave me a long hug, squeezed me tight, and said, "I knew you could do it, Murph." He always called me Murph when he was pleased with me. It was a nickname my maternal grandpa gave me when I was a day old. "She's a cute little Murph," grandpa had said, Irish slang for a potato.

Dad knew I could do it? I thought. *Wow.* I had never considered that he thought I could do things.

Mom and Dad took me out for a special dinner that night to celebrate. They talked about how great it was going to be to brag to their friends about me, and I felt so happy that they could finally do that. Usually all they had to say about me to their friends is what a problem I was, how I was so bad and such a burden. How much harder I made their lives. What a selfish daughter I was.

Now they were going to brag. About me!

I had done something excellent, and earned their love.

Later that night, I threw up the dinner in a bucket in the basement.

When I awaken again, I am on a gurney in one of the hospital hallways and my bladder is burning from fullness.

I remember the CAT scan and consider what such a test costs. My parents are going to kill me. My chest thumps in panic.

And what will my parents' friends think?

I call out for a nurse. This pee has to leave me right now, or I will explode.

"Help!" I call out. "I have to pee!"

Strangers walk by me in the hall on their way to see loved ones. Techs and nurses walk by, with looks of disgust. I close my eyes in shame. I can't not smell like hot gutter vomit.

"Please, I have to pee," I call out again.

"Hold on," says a man.

He rolls me around a corner into a doorway and pulls down my slimy jeans. He scoops me up by the bottom with one hand and places something cold and metallic beneath me. The pee splashes down my legs and into the pan. I can hear people in the hallway pass by.

The man comes back to collect the pan. He wheels me to a dark room and props my gurney up at a forty-five-degree angle.

Time passes; I don't know how much. My thoughts race.

I'm dead. I'm dead. They're going to kill me.

Or I should just kill myself.

I hear soft footsteps and feel long hair brush my face. A lady tells me to blow into a tube. I do, and she says, "Too high, Miss Erin." I feel a cold metal disc on my chest. She listens to my heart. Can she hear how much panic is there? Can a heart say such things?

She wraps my arm in a blood pressure cuff. "Forty-six," says the lady to someone else. "That's *awful* low."

My heart is always slow because I run so much.

"I run," I whisper to the lady. "When can I go home?"

"Not until your BAC is normal." Her voice is like velvet. She wipes my forehead with a warm, wet cloth.

I try to sleep, but I can't.

I'm dead. They're going to kill me. They should kill me.

⁂

I wake to a hissing noise.

It's not a snake. It's Marnie.

"You're disgusting!" says Marnie. "You fucking disgust me!"

I open my good eye and smile nervously. "Hi, Mar Mar," I say to her.

She tells me I smell and that she hates me right now. She says I am a disgrace, and asks me how I could do something like this to her.

"I know," I say. "I know, I know."

She calls me pathetic. I should pack my things, she says. Dad says I have to come home now.

Then she hisses the most terrible question:

"What will people think?" she asks. I am too sad to answer. She punctuates it with several "huh"s.

> PEOPLE WILL THINK YOU ARE WORTHLESS, ERIN. LIKE THEY ALWAYS DO. AND THEN THEY WILL THINK YOUR POOR FAMILY IS WORTHLESS TOO.

The nurse comes in from the hall and asks Marnie to return to the waiting room. They can't release me yet.

"Her heart rate is very low," says the nurse.

"I run," I whisper.

                🪐

The school places me on probation for underage drinking. I have to attend mandatory "alcohol education" classes twice a week, which I go to having freshly vomited, or run, or about to run and/or vomit. I sit cross-legged on brown, nubby carpeting in the school library with the posture of a cooked pickle and a giant black eye. I look like Spuds MacKenzie.

I draw little cartoons onto handouts with emotional gibberish on them. It makes me feel more comfortable. Or I can drift off easier, I guess.

A nice gentleman named Bob with a comb-over and high-waisted dad jeans runs the classes. He says the phrase "dangers of binge drinking" a lot. He gives us packets of papers with graphics of smiley and sad faces on them, lists of several different types of feelings and their various explanations and such.

"Quack," my dad would call him. "Head shrinker."

> **ONLY WEAK PEOPLE GO TO THERAPY, ERIN. THAT MUST BE WHY YOU'RE HERE.**

Bob says we're going to talk about the feelings that may have contributed to our binge drinking, and I cringe.

How do I tell Bob I have almost never felt the right thing?

According to witnesses, I threw myself head first down a stone stairwell. That's how I blackened my eye.

I once read that your true self comes out when you're drunk.

That same night, a freshman engineering major drank a bottle of whiskey, taped himself between two mattresses, and jumped off a balcony, collapsing one of his lungs. Then he went back up and did it again. That seems far more egregious, and yet, he is not here in these terrible classes being forced to admit he feels things.

Bob asks each of us in the group to explain our contributive emotions.

When it is my turn, I say, "Just school stress." Bob seems to think that's reasonable and moves to the next student.

The school administrators ban alcohol from the campus the following week. My new friends blame me, and I stop getting invited to parties.

The freshman engineering student with the collapsed lung never returns to school. His parents sue the university for having balconies in dorms, because it affords students the opportunity to drink, tape themselves between mattresses, and jump off. They win a settlement that is said to be quite sizable. Tuition goes up.

NOT GONNA FEEL, GONNA GO
late afternoon
RUNNING
WEST HENRIETTA BLVD.

I run every day.

I run for miles, until my knees burn. I run for hours at a time, on icy pavements, through rainstorms, when I'm sick or hung over. I run through lightning and hail. I run when it's so cold the wind makes my teeth crack and pop.

I run so I don't feel.

I get into a rhythm so I am in control. My feet go slap slap, and then I breathe.

Not going to feel it, I say to the emotion. *Not going to feel any of it. Won't feel it. Won't fucking feel you, and you can't make me,* I say. *I'm in charge now,* I say.

Slap, slap, breathe. Slap, slap, breathe.

Sometimes that doesn't work.

The feeling is there and I do my best to stop it. But it is there, and it is enormous. It sits and stews in me, and then it moves like a ninja, rising and clawing at my throat to come out like some hideous black wave.

I think:

> **IF YOU WERE A GOOD PERSON, ERIN, YOU WOULD BE CLEAN FROM THIS. IF YOU WERE STRONG, YOU WOULD BE IN CONTROL. YOU WOULDN'T NEED *ANYTHING*. YOU WOULD BE EMPTY, LIKE YOU *OUGHT* TO BE.**

When I can't hold it in, I try to find a tree I can hide behind. So no one knows. I feel everything rush out, like vomit, or diarrhea, great heaving sobs—the ugly kind, with the ugly faces and the rivers of snot running down my lip. My whole body shakes and feels weak.

Sometimes, I think I have some kind of terrible demon living inside me.

> **THAT'S WHY YOU'RE WORTHLESS, ERIN. NO CONTROL.**

I'll run more miles, to punish myself, probably.

West Henrietta Boulevard is a busy thoroughfare in Rochester. There are two lanes of traffic running in each direction, and the traffic moves rapidly—forty to fifty miles per hour. I run down West Henrietta Boulevard every day.

A few weeks have passed since my Rumple Minze party and the subsequent alien abduction. My eye has healed completely, but I still have to go see Bob for private therapy sessions. He asks me how I feel and I make something appropriate up.

It's an unseasonably warm day—perfect for running— about four in the afternoon and the light is getting flat. A car pulls up to the driveway exit of an Audi dealership I am running across. The driver looks left for oncoming traffic. I wonder if he can see me. The car starts rolling.

I wonder if I should stop running. I'm a little dizzy. *I should have eaten something today. I'm sure it will all work out.*

The car slams into the side of my leg, and—unable to stop my momentum—I end up on top of it, sliding up the hood and slamming into the windshield, behind which is a man with a look of horror on his face. He screams and hits the brakes, which sends me flying off the hood into West Henrietta Boulevard, where I land teeth-first on the asphalt. Oncoming cars screech to a halt. I see tires and the smoke of exhaust pipes and roll onto my back.

I see a lady standing over me. She asks if I am okay. I say something, but I don't know what. I don't feel so good.

She tells me I look very sweaty and asks if I'm having a heart attack.

"No," I say. "I run."

My mouth tastes like blood and feels very strange.

I run my tongue over my teeth and it catches on something rough, almost shard-like. *Shit,* I think. *Shit, shit, shit.*

My teeth are broken.

The lady presses my arms and legs, and asks if I can feel them. She puts her fingers on my neck to check my pulse and screams for someone to call an ambulance.

"I'm an EMT," she says. "You're going to be just fine."

"Well how about that," I say. I feel *very* odd.

She puts a blanket over my trunk. My vision becomes very white, and it feels nice to close my eyes, so that is what I do. This is my last memory of being in the middle of West Henrietta Boulevard.

⏮

In sixth grade, I visited the Fenton Historical Center with my classmates on a school trip. The Fenton was a stunning Italian Villa-style mansion in Jamestown, New York, where former New York Governor Reuben Fenton lived until his death in 1885.

Earlier that morning, I had begged my mother to let me wear my new pink stretch pants for the occasion. They had just come off layaway at Hills, and I planned to rock them with a geometric-block sweater in pastel purple and yellow, and flirt like hell with all the boys.

"You better not get them dirty," growled Mom, as she handed them to me.

We toured the museum, and afterward, we had the option of going out back to play in the ample English garden or partake in craft time and make candles the old way, the way they did in the 1800s. The boys went to the garden, but my best bud, Lindsay, and I could not pass up the opportunity for craft time. We went to the attic workshop and made real candles by dipping a string into a hot pot of wax and then cooling the wax that accumulated around the string in a pot of water. We repeated the process again and again—wax then water, wax then water—and after so many dips, we had candles!

My candle was lumpy and urine colored, but it was a treasure to me. When it melted on my windowsill the following July, in a rare Upstate New York heat wave, I cried.

When we were finished, Lindsay and I took our candles to the English garden behind the museum. I noticed all the cute boys were on a big hill in the back, and so I climbed that hill, cocked a hip in my sweet, pink pants, held out my candle, and proudly said, "Look at this!"

I have never been the best at being cool, or at flirting with anyone, as evidenced by what happens next—a very typical mid-flirt outcome, historically.

There was a noise in the garden behind me, and when I turned to see what it was, I tripped on a root and rolled Princess-Bride-style to the bottom of the hill. I came to a stop in a rosebush.

A parent chaperone rushed over to me. "Call an ambulance!" she said.

Wait, what? I thought, confused.

I lifted my right hand. My candle was dirty. I wiped the sticks and mud off my candle.

"Are you okay?" asked the chaperone again and again. I didn't answer. I felt funny. I think I had probably landed on my neck, because it didn't feel so good, and I was sort of dizzy.

I looked down at my legs and saw, in horror, that my brand new pink stretch pants, fresh off layaway at Hills were crusted with dirt on both knees, and on the right knee was a soul crushing, quarter-sized hole. I basically wanted to die.

"Call an ambulance," said the chaperone once more, and all sorts of panicked thoughts ran through my head.

How much did an ambulance cost? My god, my mother will be angry enough about my stretch pants. We can't afford things like ambulance rides. We can't even afford the co-pay thingy. Whatever that is. Mom is always saying "THE CO-PAY!"

"No!" I screamed. "No, I am fine!"

The co-pay, for Christ's sake!

My mother was in the kitchen reading a *People Magazine* when I got home from school that day. She looked up at me, down to my knee, and back up again. I felt like I might shit myself, and made a desperate appeal for sympathy. "I fell and hurt myself," I said. "I think I twisted my neck."

"WHAT DID YOU DO TO YOUR STRETCH PANTS?"

There was an ambulance ride, they tell me. I got here by ambulance. I don't remember it. I must be in some sort of shock. *How much does an ambulance ride cost, for shit's sake?*

HOW MUCH DOES A FUCKING AMBULANCE RIDE COST?

I'm dead. They're going to kill me.

What would my parents' friends think of my broken teeth? Oh, the money my parents spent on my braces. No, the fortune they spent on my braces! The absolute fucking fortune!

And THE PICTURES!

I'll look like a hillbilly in the family pictures!

I am awash with guilt. I am shame itself.

That's it; they're going to kill me.

The nice nurse with the velvet voice comes into the examination room. "Hello, Erin," she says, with a look of concern. She asks me questions, and they don't make sense to me. When I answer the questions, she is confused and asks me more questions.

My body feels very cold and I'm dizzy.

She takes my blood pressure and frowns. Too low, she says. "Bradycardia," she says. I don't know what that means.

She shines a flashlight into my eyes and must see something there, because she puts her hand on top of mine like my dog just died or something.

Her hand feels soft.

There is a band of connective tissue that runs down the outsides of legs, holding muscle, bone, and tissue in place. It is called an "iliotibial band," and I have bruised mine, or traumatized it in some way. I can't run for a month. I banged my head up pretty good and broke my teeth, but these are my only injuries.

But the hospital bill is big and my parents are not happy about that, plus it will cost quite a bit to fix my broken teeth so that I look appropriate in pictures again.

Mom seems most angry about the teeth.

"Your perfect teeth!" she says. "All the money we spent to fix them."

"Get your shit together," says dad.

There's a set of train tracks by campus that runs deep into the woods. It's a little spooky, if I'm being honest.

The tracks are abandoned and in a state of disrepair, and I can only run down them by hopping down the middle slats in a rhythm, chanting or counting to keep my stride consistent. If I don't do this, my feet miss the slats and I hit the rocks between and twist my ankle.

I run and count, like a crazy person. The rhythm feels oddly pleasant. I experience less of my rogue-wave shit crying incidents when I count my pace on the train tracks.

But there is the problem of the rickety bridge, of course, that goes over the Genesee River. Instead of running on wood slats, one has to deal with a rickety-at-best metal grate, and the bridge wobbles underfoot. I often wonder if I should even be running over it, but run over it I do. And often, I am so dizzy. *I should eat before I run,* I think. Or I should abstain from stuffing myself with ice cream and then ripping it back out before running.

Halfway across the bridge, the toe of one of my sneakers gets wedged between two metal grates and I fall.

I stand and brush the dirt from my shorts, streaking them with blood from my cut palms. I am angry because I just bought these shorts with my summer waitressing money. My knee is burning and looks pretty bad. It's been sliced into a waffle pattern from the metal grate and chunks of skin seem to be hanging from my kneecap.

That's not good, I think. I feel very weird again. I consider I should go back to the hospital, but think this might also be dramatic. I decide I will run back to my dorm and buy some Band-Aids or something.

I run my way out of the woods and through a residential area, being sure to not look down. There's a man mowing his yard, and when he sees me, he turns his mower off and rushes over. He says some things to me that I don't remember. I feel very dizzy now.

He seems to think I have hurt myself, so I tell him I am fine. I simply need to buy some Band-Aids.

"Wait right here," he says, running into his house for a towel. He spreads the towel across the back seat of his car and helps me into it, elevating my leg across the seat. There's a bright sheen of blood on my shin, and my right shoe and sock are soaked and deeply red. My eyes are starting to get white again and my thoughts are quite strange.

He drops me off at the entrance to the emergency room.

How much do stitches cost? I think.

SHIT!

The doctor at the emergency room does his best. He explains that I have turned my knee to "hamburger" and there's little he can do to put it back together. I watch as he stitches some of the chunks to some of the other chunks. It's a very strange thing to witness.

He wraps my leg in an immobilizer that I am instructed to wear for a month.

"There's nothing that can be done about the scars," he says.

I'm dead. They're going to kill me.

"**R**ichard! Rush the growler," he'd say. Maybe he'd say it with a gruff kind of smoker's voice, and maybe he was playing poker at a table with other grizzled old farm people with equally gruff voices. I don't really know, because I never met my great grandpa.

I try to imagine I am there watching. I try to go back there as much as I can, if only to understand, and of course, to feel close to him. But I only know these few things—this little story, the details of his wardrobe, the phrase "rush the growler"—from snooping through old photo albums and spying on my father when he talks to others. He will tell me little to nothing about his past.

I know Dad was only a boy, not even six years old. I have seen photos, so I know he had fine, sandy-colored hair and Irish eyes that slimmed to half moons when he smiled. I know he wore hand-sewn overalls with hand-me-down buttons, and that the family was exceedingly poor, but proud and hardworking.

I don't have to imagine what the family farmhouse looked like, because I had been there so many times—every Christmas Eve, some Easters, but never any other day just because. It was a modest little house on a windswept hill in Oswego, New York, a port city on Lake Ontario. It had been a working farm back then, and the family made extra scratch during the summer selling blocks of ice. *Did my father sell ice? They must have had refrigerators in the forties.*

I try to imagine the barn that isn't in the yard anymore. I imagine animals. I don't even know what kind of farm it was, but I imagine animals anyway—sometimes cows, and sometimes chickens. Sometimes I imagine a few pigs and piglets.

I imagine it was very cold. This is the only way I know this place to be, perpetually blanketed in a thick layer of lake-effect snow, softening every sharp edge. It must be summer there, sometimes, but it seems strange to imagine it this way.

So Dad, just a tiny boy, grabs the growler from the table the old men play cards at. *How big is the growler? It must be almost as big as he is, and does he struggle to carry it?* I imagine, yes. He carries it to the front door and sets it on the floor. He finds his leather boots—which have to have holes in them—and shoves his feet into them. Maybe there are holes in his hand-knit woolen socks too. This will be a cold walk. *Does anyone help him tie his boots, or does he do it himself?* I could tie my shoes at six, but then, my parents coached me through it with the talk of the "bunny ears" and going "around the tree," and when I couldn't figure it out, there was no slap on the head or mention of me being stupid. I can't imagine my grandparents doing it the same way. *Was there time for these tender conversations? Or energy?* They were lucky to eat. They were blessed to be alive. It was a miracle they didn't starve to death, or end up bleeding out on a beach in the South Pacific, only sixteen and poked full of more holes than a piece of Swiss cheese.

He puts on a red-and-black checked coat made of wool and a leather cap with earflaps. I have seen the coat and hat in photos, so this imagining is verifiable. He hugs the growler to his chest with mittened hands and heads out into the cold.

Its dark, and the snow is thick, sucking at his boots as he lifts his feet to stomp down the road.

Why is this happening? He's only six.

The corner store is not actually on the corner. It is nearly a mile up the road. His nose and toes are numb when he gets there; his mittens stick to the frost on the side of the growler.

The old man or old lady who owns the store fills the growler with beer, charges Great Grandpa's account for the cost, and sends Dad back out into the snow. It's darker now. The jug is heavier now, and there's another mile to walk.

It's cold and he's alone.

I'd be lying if I said there was anything I ever wanted more than to be there with him. I wanted to walk with him, and to hold his hand. I wanted to carry the growler. I wanted to button up his coat and help him through the snow. I wanted to hold him by his shoulders, look deeply into his sweet blue eyes, and say, "You will be loved," because in twenty-four years I will be born, and it will be so profoundly true. I will love him with the fire of a thousand suns, and he will never notice it.

But I can't do any of these things, because time is cruel and it only goes one way. I have no sway in 1954.

SO, THIS IS
CHRISTMAS

—

OSWEGO, NY, -8 DEGREES

It's a few months later, midafternoon on Christmas Eve. We are driving to my paternal grandparents' house to celebrate the holiday with family.

I am in the back seat of the family station wagon, anxious and hung over, head pounding from too many secret sips of kitchen cabinet liquors—mixed in whatever way I could get them when nobody was looking. I'm wearing a new cable-knit sweater and a new pair of leather boots mom and Dad got me for Christmas, and a slightly intense shade of pink lipstick that feels waxy and terrible on my mouth. I don't like makeup, but Mom says I really need it.

I'm gazing out the window of the station wagon, worrying and picking at my cuticles. I pick too hard, and one begins to bleed a bit. My stomach is churning with the wrong emotions—fear, anxiety, anger—instead of all the correct feelings a girl ought to feel while wearing expensive presents with one's perfect family on Christmas Eve, on the way to one's grandmother's house.

My parents have been cold and distant over the break. I suspect they are enraged about my disastrous first semester—the medical bills and the social embarrassment—but no one has said as much. The lack of conversation about the matter only causes me more anxiety. It feels as if the tension is building into something terrible. My father's body is constipated with anger, I can tell. He sneers at me as he walks past, and spends long hours in the basement buffing his guns.

I wish we could go back in time to the day I got my scholarship, when Dad was beaming, and it seemed he might love me. It wasn't that long ago. *Can I remind him? Can we go back?*

I announce to the car that I got A's in all my classes, hoping it will dilute the tension. I cannot be that bad a daughter if I got all A's in my classes.

Silence.

I talk about fonts and colors, and everything I have learned about them. No one responds, so I talk about the fancy things I learned about shapes and space to fill up our space with something other than my worry. "Hey Dad," I say. "Did you know that what you don't put into a design is just as important as what you *do* put into it?"

He grumbles.

"Huh? Did you know that?"

Silence.

> REAL JOBS ARE MATH AND SCIENCE JOBS, ERIN. BUT YOU CAN'T DO MATH, BECAUSE YOU'RE FUCKING STUPID.

We stop for lunch at a greasy spoon. Marnie and Mom talk about girly stuff and I sit and stare at my plate, my heart fluttering up or down at the sound of Dad's sighs. Every moment we don't speak feels like a prelude to something violent.

We get back into the car to finish our drive. I gaze out the window for a while, and when I can't take the silence anymore, I begin to talk again, about all the things I learned at school that semester.

I talk about serifs, those little feet on fonts, and how that can express all sorts of meanings. I talk about how my typography teacher left me a note on my final project. "Erin, you are so talented," it had said.

"Hear that, Dad? He said I was so talented."

"That's it!" screams Dad, slamming on the brakes. The car skids to a shaky halt.

"You are not special, Erin!" he screams into the windshield. "YOU ARE NOT SPECIAL."

His hands grip the steering wheel in an ugly, sinewy grip, and Mom places a concerned hand on his knee, but says nothing.

Marnie says nothing.

I look out the window into the snow. I wonder how I could have been so stupid, so selfish. The farmhouse looms ahead on the right side of the road, puffy with lake-effect snow.

> **YOU ARE NOT SPECIAL, ERIN. YOU ARE NOTHING AT ALL. NOTHING.**

It has snowed in Oswego. It's always snowing in Oswego.

I think it must snow there in June.

There's a fluff of pleasant crystals on every branch of every tree, on the wires that bring the electricity to the farmhouse, on the shutters and eaves and on the toolshed roof in which Great Uncle Ray shot himself in the face.

I give hugs to my family, smiling with closed lips, so they don't see my teeth.

I hover in the living room for a bit and skim through a *National Geographic* magazine about the finding of the Titanic on the mint brocade couch. Then I eat a few potato chips and one sugar cookie from a table in the living room. I'm trying to make my way to the alcohol without anyone noticing. When the path is clear, I go to the cases of beer on the porch to sneak one. I cover my palm in my new cable knit sweater, uncap the beer, and gulp it down as quickly as I can.

There's a retching noise by the garage. Uncle Mark is vomiting behind it. He stands up, wipes his mouth, and looks my way. He sees me holding the beer and we two share an unspoken understanding, which I interpret as this: *I will tell no one I saw you vomiting behind the garage and you will tell no one I am drinking beer.*

I walk back inside and notice Dad in a circle of uncles with a mug, grinning and telling jokes. I know the mug has "Wild Coffee" in it, which is what Dad calls straight Wild Turkey in a coffee mug. They begin to play their game of joke brinksmanship, tossing verbal assaults back and forth, having waited all year to reconvene in this house and say to each other the equivalent of: *You're worthless, har har.*

Which of them will be broken, and run away in tears? I've never seen such a thing, to be honest. They all win at this game. They are *incredibly* good at this game. They take a verbal punch full in the face, swallow it, and do nothing more than bare their teeth in aggressive chimp smiles. Then they strike back, and strike even harder. Oh, they are *very* good at this game.

But it's "just jokes," as Dad says when he plays this game with me and I tell him it hurts. "You're too sensitive. It's just jokes, Erin."

I walk around the old farmhouse looking at family photos, touching the antiques, trying to pick up visual and energetic clues. There are old toys from the forties in the den. There's a bowl full of coins from Europe on an end table. There's a mass-produced, dusty still life on a wall—a table, some cheese, a candle, and a red apple with a knife, the only pop of color in the house. Everything else is an array of brown, or some relative of brown—ochre, beige, mustard, acorn. The people are wearing brown, and their hair is brown. By the door, there's a pile of brown shoes and boots.

Grandma is in the kitchen, chain smoking and reading a book. I won't go in there. The aunts and other womenfolk usually gather at the dining room table and sometimes Grandma makes an appearance to refill the crystal bowl of potato chips and make weirdly tangential statements like "I'm glad I only had *male* children."

I sneak more beer.

We eat dinner, spaghetti.

It is now very late, and Dad seems to have had too much Wild Coffee. It's funny—Dad doesn't really drink much, except for Christmas Eve. He's telling everyone a "fun story" he says, about what I did this most recent semester at college, how I am a drunk and how I've been in and out of the hospital, and what an embarassment I am.

When my uncles are done belly laughing at my expense, one suggests my college name the alcohol ban the "Erin Tyler Memorial Ban on Alcohol."

I try to make my face unmovable, though I feel terrible sadness inside. I can't show this, because we are playing the game and I can't have them thinking I am sensitive and I don't have a good sense of humor. Wait, *are we playing the game, or am I feeling the wrong things again?* I never can tell. I'll just bare my teeth.

"That's another thing," says Dad. "She broke her teeth."

Everyone roars, and I'm not sure why. That's not a joke. It's not even funny; it's just a statement of fact. *What is this game?*

I go for a potato chip and another cookie. I hear him say "my asshole daughter" from the living room. I hear big laughs. *Is that funny? Simply calling your daughter an asshole? What a lazy joke.*

I mean, a *joke* would be like:

> Q: WHAT'S BLACK AND WHITE AND RED ALL OVER?
>
> A: MY BORDERLINE CRAZY ASSHOLE DAUGHTER AFTER SHE THREW HERSELF DOWN A STONE STAIRWELL.

Now that would be a joke—not a good joke, but at least it's within the realm of jokehood, structurally speaking. At least there's a fucking punchline.

I drink more beer behind the house. It's colder now. The cold helps me feel numb. The air is thick with floating flakes, and the roof of the woodshed is swollen and puffy. The crystals sparkle in the light. When I breathe in through my nose, I can feel my snot freeze to my nose hairs.

I wonder what kind of gun Ray used.

It's four o'clock, and I *hate* four o'clock.

My mother will be home soon.

Marnie is hiding in her room, her nose in a book about some dumb girl with dumb problems, and how she finally managed to become pretty. The house is cold and blue inside. It's wintertime, and the darkness comes early now. I am watching television but not really paying much attention to it, digging a pair of nippers into my cuticles, which are a little bloody. It hurts and I should stop doing it, but I don't.

I hop off the sofa and wander around, prickles of panic climbing my limbs. I go to the den and pull an encyclopedia out. I read a page or two on my knees on the floor in the corner where Dad sits and reads his spy novels. It's the coldest corner in the whole house.

My mind drifts, and I wonder what the problem with me will be today. *What about me is incorrect, or bad, or burdensome? How have I disappointed her? Have I not done enough at school? Have I not done my hair correctly? Have I eaten junk food? Nobody likes fat people. Have I done something that costs her money? Do I have a pimple? Have I been thinking the wrong, sassy, uppity things—the things she doesn't think or say—or feeling the wrong feelings? Have I done anything she could brag about to her friends? How do I compare to their children? Do I add up? Have I not put things back into their places, the places she says they ought to be, just the way she likes things to be, at just the right angles that defuse her? Have I been using her nippers when I know I shouldn't be using her nippers, when I know I am under no circumstances permitted to use her goddamn nippers?*

Shit.

I go back to the living room and put the nippers in the "nipper place" inside the nipper drawer. I tilt them so that the points are to the left like the tweezers—handle right, points left. I sigh a little and close the drawer.

That was a close one.

I go upstairs and dig my fingers into my nose, watching white gunk slide out of my pores. I'm greasy and gross now, a monster in mid-transition. Mom doesn't like my skin, and

I don't either. Mom's friends' daughters have better skin and hair—they have thinner waistlines and don't sass people or say weird things.

YOU'RE SO UGLY, ERIN.

There's a new voice in my head these days. It says that I am bad and worthless. Well, it isn't new, I suppose, because it has been there for years, but lately it has risen up and it tells me I am fat and ugly. It says I am stupid and lazy, and that I will never be good enough. No one will ever love me.

At night, I spend hours standing in front of the mirror in my bedroom, judging myself to be the ugliest creature alive. I squeeze the fat on my upper arms and legs until it reddens and bruises.

My body is changing and people don't like me anymore. My breath smells. My armpits reek, says Mom. My face grows red lumps, volcanic in size, and slicks with grease that has to be wiped away three or more times a day. My nipples are weirdly puffy, but not real breasts, and nowhere near as big as my mom's friends' daughters' breasts, which are superior to mine. The boys at school say I'm the president of the Itty Bitty Titty Committee.

Dad barely speaks to me anymore.

My nose begins to bleed a little, so I pat a piece of toilet paper into the blood puddle like Dad does when he cuts himself shaving. The paper turns red and sticks there.

YOU'RE A MONSTER, ERIN.

I don't hear you, voice! I can't hear you, I say. *You're a mean old voice. La la la. I will dance now.*

I'll pretend you aren't there!

I practice a few arabesques and some kicks in the bathroom mirror. Marnie says I suck at dancing. She says I dance like an ox. Marnie is much better at dancing than I am. I do some spins down the upstairs hallway, get dizzy, and topple into a framed family portrait, tilting it, slightly. "Uh oh," I say, fixing it carefully, perpendicular to the molding at just the right angle Mom likes things to be. I stand back and check my work.

Is it good enough? It's not good enough. Nothing is ever good enough.

I lie down on my bed and stare at the wall. It's a mostly purple wall with one half-finished, hand-painted sunflower in the middle of it, an attempt at a mural that I abandoned half way through. I should finish it, I think. I can make it better, I think. A bad feeling melts through my stomach as I examine it. I screwed up one of the petals on the top right side of the flower, and then I panicked and painted over it again and again to try to make it right. The bright yellow I was using for the light parts of the petal started to get muddy with the brown I was using to give the petals depth with shading, and then I decided I had no talent and I should die. Now the thing sits there in a purple void and mocks me.

I once got a spinner toy in an egg from a prize machine at the skating rink. It had a little handle on top of it and if you twisted the handle hard enough, it would spin for twenty, maybe thirty seconds. There was a bright red spiral painted on the top of it, and when it started rotating, the spiral would swirl and swirl. The boys at school liked to flick it with their fingers just to mess with me, and when they did that, the spinner would wobble and twist and fall down. Sometimes it would spin right off my desk and onto the floor.

I feel like that lately. I feel like something flicked me and now my spin is off.

I wonder what time it is? It must be after five now.

Maybe I should play some music, I think. *I love music.*

I run downstairs to the stereo, pop a cassette into the deck, close it, and hit play. My cold blue house is full of INXS now. It's not so cold or blue now. I dance around the living room like a sexy older lady from a video with breasts of an appropriate size, swinging my hips back and forth beneath an appropriately sized waistline. I don't feel like me anymore: gross and bad and burdensome.

No, I feel *happy*.

The music is loud, and I don't the hear rocks crack under the weight of her car in the driveway. Nor do I hear the sound of a car door being slammed shut in a way that could be referred to as dramatic. I don't hear Mom's rubber soles stomp up the back steps and into the house, nor the slamming of the back door in a manner that one could call histrionic.

I do not hear her boots land against the wall of the mudroom in two frustrated thuds.

Oh, but I definitely hear—in my head, heart, and bowels—the thunderous exclamation "TURN THAT MUSIC OFF!"

It is one year later, the fall semester of my second year away at school.

I am a very troubled young woman, having spent my summer break drinking to excess, punishing myself with exercise, and vomiting every night into a bucket in the basement of my parents' home. I have dated three idiot abusers in masochistic succession, and spoken to myself in such a cruel and abusive manner that there were many days I was not able to summon enough will to leave the living room sofa.

I loathe myself more than ever before.
I believe I am more of a disappointment to
my family than I ever have been.

In just a few short weeks I'll nearly die again—
this time *quite* intentionally—and after that, two
magical things will happen:

1. I'LL HAVE MY FIRST *RATIONAL* THOUGHT
ABOUT MY SELF AND MY FAMILY, AND

2. I'LL MEET MY FIRST LOVE.

I will never try to kill myself again.

MUSHROOM TEA
RIT·FALL·'98

I am dressed in warm clothes—in overalls, boots, and a sweater—struggling to pull my pants down so I can pee in the girls' bathroom on my old dorm room floor. I don't live on campus anymore. I live in an apartment a few miles north of campus, and I rarely visit anymore. But Beth said we had to do mushrooms.

"It's a spiritual experience," she had said.

I am yanking at my sweater, but it won't come off, no matter how hard I pull. I am banging my elbows against the sides of the stall and laughing. *Why is this so hard?*

"What the hell are you doing in there?" asks Beth from outside the stall.

"I can't get my sweater off," I say. "It's stuck to me."

"It's not stuck to you," says Beth. "You're wearing overalls over your sweater, dummy."

"Oh," I say, giggling.

The mushrooms are kicking in. Beth said they take thirty minutes or so to do that. We got them from Adrian, the curly blond boy with the green jacket who gets people anything they want. Beth cut them up and boiled them in her coffee pot with three bags of tea we took from the dining hall so the tea wouldn't taste so bad.

"You have to make tea," she says. "You can't eat them, or you'll get sick."

Beth is very sexy. I met her at a Halloween party during my disastrous first semester, to which she wore black leather pants and a headband with red horns on it. I knew who she was, because nobody liked her and all the girls talked shit about her. They said she was too full of herself and that she liked to beat girls up on the lacrosse field. I figured since nobody liked me either, I should be friends with her.

Beth knows nobody likes her, and somehow doesn't care. "Fuck them," she says. I can't imagine not caring what people think of me. What people think of me consumes my thoughts. I can literally think of nothing else.

The mushroom tea is strong, and by the time I'm done peeing

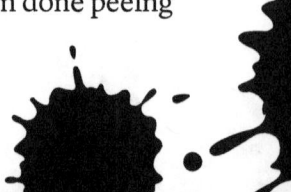

I need Beth's help to put my overalls back together.

"I feel weird," I say to Beth. There are swirly patterns on the walls of the bathroom, and swirly patterns on my face in the mirror.

"You're supposed to feel weird," says Beth. "That's the point."

Beth and I head out into the cold in our layers of warm clothes. Beth says you have to be outside in nature when you do mushrooms.

We walk down the quarter mile hand in hand. My nose itches in the cold air, and I giggle and scratch it.

Beth stops and looks up. "Whoa," she says. "Look at the colors." I look up too, but I don't see colors. I see the stars are moving around in swirly patterns like the walls in the bathroom. How had I never noticed them moving before?

Beth and I walk around campus, inspecting things. We pick up leaves, hold them up to the light, and Beth says they are incredible. A raccoon spills out of a dumpster behind the dining hall and we chase it into the woods. "Wait!" yells Beth as it disappears into the dark.

"I want to be your friend!" I say.

We do somersault runs down a hill, but I get too dizzy and feel like I might vomit.

Beth wants to go to Adrian's fraternity to play Ping-Pong in the basement. I don't want to go there. "Let's stay out here," I say to her.

"Its getting cold," says Beth. "C'mon, it will be fun."

The basement is cold and dark, and I am a little frightened. I cling to a pole while Beth turns on the lights and finds a ball and two paddles. I join Beth at the table and we play a little. I can't seem to hit the ball back to Beth. When it comes over the net, it becomes many balls, and I don't know which one to send back to her. Beth laughs as I swing wildly at nothing. "Which one is it?" I yell.

Beth is crippled with laughter. "You're so fucked up," she says, setting her paddle down on the table and taking my hand. "Let's go see Adrian," she says.

I don't want to go see Adrian, but I don't say it. I do not like Adrian.

Beth leads me to a stairwell and I tell her I cannot go up. The stairwell has teeth and I will die if I go into it. Beth says the stairwell does not have teeth; I am simply on mushrooms and I am hallucinating.

"We can do this," she says, placing my hands on her hips.

We walk very slowly up the stairs. I hold on to Beth and try to not look at the teeth. The walls are wiggly and then they turn into waves. Little fish with long, pretty tails jump in the waves. We go up and up, my hands on Beth's hips. She has nice hips. The fish jump in the wall waves.

We reach the top of the stairs and turn the corner. "See, that wasn't so hard," says Beth.

We hear beeps and radio noises at the end of the hallway, where two policemen are standing next to a frightened boy. His hands are zip-tied behind his back.

Then a horrible thing happens: I feel all the wrong things, all at once, all the sorrow, the panic, the rage, and the self-loathing. Every last bit of me fills with terrible feelings that run amok.

I cannot stand anymore, so I slump to the floor.

MUSHROOM TEA | 74

"No," I say, pressing my face into my hands. "No."

"Get up!" hisses Beth.

"No," I say.

"Stay here," whispers Beth, disappearing down the hall.

I rock back and forth and say "no."

No, no, no, no...

The feelings rip through me, and I cannot stop them.

I see two brown shoes and some legs. Adrian squats down and peels my hands from my face. "Come with me, now" he whispers, pulling me up from the floor.

He puts his arm around my shoulders and pulls me into his room.

"Is she okay?" asks Beth.

"She'll be fine," says Adrian.

I am not fine. I have never been less fine. I feel it all. I feel everything.

I want to die.

A terrible boy comes into the room, sees me on the bed, and laughs. "She's freaking out!" he says. He thinks this is hilarious. "Let's make her watch that Aphex Twin video," he says.

"Fuck off," says Beth.

I stay the night here on Adrian's stinky bed, bound up in a sweaty ball, my arms tightly gripped around my knees. The feelings come in horrible waves that eventually subside, and when I get sleepy and drift off, I have a nightmare of being bit in half by a giant shark.

My head is pounding. It is the dead of night and I am back in Adrian's room, on Adrian's stinky bed, but I don't know how I got here.

I smell a mixture of liquor and something sweet like grape punch and remember I had been at a party. Adrian had been there, and he had given me a cup, which I drank as fast as I could. I don't remember anything after that.

My shirt is twisted around my torso and cutting into my skin. I reach down to straighten it and feel my chest. My bra is unhooked but still over my shoulders. My shirt has been opened and buttoned back up again, incorrectly. My jeans are down below my hips, the fly open.

My belly feels slightly sticky, as if something disgusting had landed there and then been quickly wiped away by an asshole.

Adrian is sleeping on a sofa across the room. I can hear the buzzing of his mini fridge. He stirs a little, rolls over, and starts to snore again.

Oh, you fucking pig.

I sit up on the bed and re-button my shirt. I find my shoes in the dark, creep to the door, and open it slowly so it doesn't creak. The light from the hallway brightens the room a little and I catch a glimpse of Adrian's green army surplus jacket tossed over the arm of his sofa. I slide my hand into one of the pockets and steal everything in it.

Fucking pig.

I wander around the student lot in the cold, searching the rows for my car. I can't remember where it's parked, and my brain feels strange again—not because of the pounding in my head. It feels strangely like it did in the middle of West Henrietta Boulevard, or when I fell on the bridge and my vision turned oddly white. My thoughts are not orderly, and I can't quite grab on to to them.

And the mean old voice in my head that tells me I'm nothing is very loud tonight.

WHAT A WHORE YOU ARE, ERIN.

☠ ☠ ☠

Up until now I thought that most of my problems in life could be solved if I could make all of my feelings go away.

I believed if there was some sort of pill or patch—some miracle of modern medicine—that would make me feel empty, I could be so much more functional. I could focus on being excellent for my family, and if I didn't feel anything at all, then I couldn't burden them all the time with my incorrect feelings.

But it turns out I was wrong. I was very, very wrong.

Now I don't feel anything, and it is the worst feeling I have ever had.

I don't go anywhere. I throw up three times a day. I am puffy and gray-faced, and I spend all day lying on the sofa watching shapes move on the television without the slightest care about the plot. It's all just noise. My face buzzes with a strange, unpleasant energy that feels like the internal equivalent of nails on a chalkboard.

Sometimes I run at night, if I can, for hours at a time—twelve, seventeen, even twenty miles, down foreign streets, in cemeteries, in woods, and through poverty-crippled neighborhoods where gangs war for turf, where fifty-person gang fights happen on abandoned lots between "reds" and "yellows," as best as one could assess from the clothing worn. I run through it, and I feel nothing.

Nada. *Zip.*

Some days I cannot run, and can barely do anything at all apart from one exhausting and necessary trip to a store to buy food to eat and then vomit back up. Sometimes I don't shower for four or five days and when the phone rings, I can't fathom answering it. How had I ever done such a horrifying thing as answering a phone?

I haven't been to campus for a month. I must be failing every class, but I do not care.

My throat has a hole in it from the various objects I scrape against the back of it to get the food out. My teeth have holes in the backs of them, and my knuckles are covered in scabs. My knees scream from the running, and from the vomiting too. Bulimia makes one's knees feel like napalm.

If I pass a mirror, I want to punch it.

The answering machine picks up. It's my cousin, Evan. His father—my Uncle Mark—is coming in for parents' weekend, and he's calling to invite me out to dinner, out of obligation more than desire, I suspect.

Evan goes to RIT, too, but we never see each other.

I call him back and tell him I have to work. It's a lie. In truth, I could barely return his call, let alone shower, drive to a restaurant full of people, eat food without a place to vomit and chit-chat for hours with two relatives who rightfully loathe me.

I haven't been to work in weeks. I must be fired by now.

I wonder if my bank account is overdrawn.

☠ ☠ ☠

It is 4 a.m.

I am too tired to be certain, but I think I have been awake for two days. Time is hard to understand now.

My joints throb, and my face aches. My cheeks are burning.

There's the energy of a scream or a bomb behind my face and if either went off, they would rip my throat to shreds.

The smell of rotten food is on my fingers, and I cannot get it off no matter how many times I wash my hands.

I think I have stress fractures in my shins. It hurts when I press them, when I stand on tiptoes or step down from curbs.

I do have stress fractures. They won't heal for several years.

People make faces on the television.

☠ ☠ ☠

It is a cold, rainy night. Higher patches of West Henrietta Boulevard are frozen over and slick under the tires of my car. I am driving home from the store with food I won't digest. The car heater isn't working very well, and I am shivering in my seat.

I am not wearing a coat. I thought about putting one on, but it felt too complicated or exhausting. I'd have to open the closet door and tango with the other coats and their hangers. There would be buttons and zippers. It seemed like a lot of effort.

The sky is blackened with clouds I can't see. Streetlights hover in the rain, which is so thick their poles are undetectable. They look like tiny UFOs hovering on alternate sides of the road. There's a large truck heading toward me in one of the opposite lanes.

> **YOU SHOULD TURN INTO THE TRUCK, ERIN. IF YOU HAD GUTS, YOU WOULD.**

I don't.

☠ ☠ ☠

I am nervous, which is the first legitimate feeling I have felt in a long time.

I set the whiskey on the coffee table. *Should I get a glass?* It doesn't really matter, I guess.

I pull the plastic off the cap with my teeth and unscrew the bottle. The whiskey tastes horrible and I wonder why Dad even likes it.

The hole in my throat briefly burns, and then I feel warm all over my body.

I set the baggie of pills on the coffee table next to the whiskey. Mom used to put snacks into little baggies like this for me to take to school, way back when Mom didn't hate me. I don't know what kind of pills they are or if they are even pills, only that they were in Adrian's front pocket, and knowing Adrian, this meant they were illegal and would probably do the trick. "Do the trick," I am calling it. Somehow it feels better to say it that way. Of course, I don't know that any of this will work, but I don't have the guts to turn my car into a truck, and I could never use a shotgun like Uncle Ray did.

I swallow the pills in little clusters washed down with whiskey, which takes more time than I had imagined when I thought about all this. I may get warmer and warmer, but the whiskey never gets any tastier.

Gah, how does Dad drink this?

When I'm done, I don't know what else to do, so I sit back and look around. I rub my legs and try to calm myself. *Things will be okay soon*, I think. I'll go away and everybody's lives will be better. I won't have to be me anymore. I can float off to some other plane of existence and be someone or something else entirely.

Of course, I don't know if that's true, really. *Wouldn't it be a terrible irony if I left here and went somewhere else, and I had to be me there as well?*

I lean back on the sofa and try not to think such things. I feel quite drunk now. I don't know why, but it seems like a good idea to play some music. *I like music.*

I have *always* liked music.

This is all I remember.

A day passes, and I awaken on the same old plane of existence, the same shitty person.

I am on my back in the middle of my living room, gazing at the popcorn ceiling of my apartment. There are about a hundred or more broken CD cases strewn about my person. I assume I must have slept somewhat fitfully on the pills and whiskey—pushing my limbs up and down many times—because I have created a sort of vomit-and-CD-case angel on the cheap green Berber carpeting of my living room.

Nearby is a CD rack, which is ordinarily mounted to the wall above the television, and it, too, is strewn about in pieces, having been violated somehow.

there's a smelly halo of whiskey and pill paste around my head, in my hair, and dried in a crust on both of my cheeks.

I'll never really know what happened when I got up to play music, or even what kind of music I wanted to play at the time—which I've actually thought about quite a bit—and I will never know what those pills were.

They could have been opiates or barbiturates, or any other kinds of drugs rapey creeps use to sedate people.

Of course, they could have been nothing more than curiously strong peppermints for all I know.

I am eating ice cream in the back of the campus library, hiding cross-legged under a table like a dog with something it stole from the dinner table.

I'm paging through a history of New York City, fascinated by the conditions of the slums and immigrant neighborhoods, and that anyone could have survived them. I wonder if my ancestors ever lived there.

I have always liked libraries and books in general. Everything about books makes me feel alive.

There is truth in books. There are facts and things you can rely upon that don't change on mood-based whims.

Of all the buildings at school, I spend the most time here, in the library. I read for hours and eat my meals here. I sneak into dark corners in the stacks and nibble at pretzels, reading about the Civil War, Vikings, plagues, and schools of thought. I read classic literature and collections of poetry. I love Anne Sexton and Chuck Bukowski. I *love* T.S. Eliot.

LIKE A PATIENT ETHERIZED UPON A TABLE.

I don't read about design, though. I don't give a fuck about it.

I'm still just a student, but design is disappointing. It seems to me like an art form of promoting others, not the self, and though I seem to be quite good at it—and almost preternaturally gifted at melting myself down and diving into the needs of others, if only to make *them* feel fantastic about *them*—the work leaves me feeling empty. Even in these days, when I should be optimistic, and I take any odd job that comes my way to build a portfolio, design makes me feel sad and empty, like I've taken a huge, painful shit for no reason.

I never wanted to be a designer. I wanted to be an artist, but Mom said her friends thought artists were weird, and that I would probably not be good enough to make any money.

YOU HAVE TO MAKE LOTS OF MONEY IF YOU'RE GOING TO BE HAPPY IN LIFE. YOU HAVE TO BUY STUFF, AND STUFF COSTS MONEY.

I finish my pint of ice cream and close my book about New York. I drop the spoon into the empty cup and slide the book back into the stacks.

I make my way to the bathroom and pull a Sharpie out of my book bag. I stab it into the back of my throat and the ice cream flies out in several big whooshes. My knees start to scream in protest. Stop doing that, they say. We don't like that.

I flush the toilet and scoop some water into my mouth to rinse out the vomit. I am washing snot off my face when I hear my name over the loudspeaker. "Erin Tyler, please come to the reception desk."

I wonder if you can get into trouble for puking.

I head to the reception desk and sheepishly say I am Erin. The receptionist says I have a phone call, and hands me the telephone.

"Hello," I say into the receiver.

"Erin," says Meg, my sister's college roommate who lives nearby. "I've been looking for you." She seems very upset about something.

"Can you come to my house?" asks Meg.

"Yes," I say. "What is this about?"

"I better not say until you get here," she says.

Meg gives me a long hug at her door, petting my back in gentle circles as if I am a puppy or she feels sorry for me. It feels uncomfortable.

She ushers me into her kitchen and sits me down. "Do you want some tea?" she asks. I tell her no, I don't.

I just want to know what I did wrong this time.

She reaches across the kitchen table for my hand, and I give it to her.

"Your Uncle Mark killed himself," she says.

The FUNERAL
OSWEGO, NY

Three Days Later

I am hovering over my Uncle Mark's dead body, listening to Phil Collins's "Sussudio."

I always thought Mark was the handsomest of his brothers; he looks good. He's a bit swollen in his pleasant, brown suit—his slightly puffed hands stacked onto his barrel chest—but all in all, he's a handsome dead man, which only adds to my confusion.

The air smells of both chemicals and flowers, and his body and coffin are lit up with hot-pink disco light that seems inappropriately saturated for such an occasion.

There's a girl that's been on my mind. I think about her all the time.

Su su sudio. Oh oh.

She don't even know my name, but I think she loves me just the same...

Here come the horns. *What a wretched song.*

Mark had left a letter behind, and in it, he asked that we listen to Phil Collins's *Hits* at his funeral. I think he was more imagining that we'd begin saying our goodbyes to the dramatic and powerful "In the Air Tonight," striking a tone more like the finale of a somber episode of *Miami Vice* he must have watched and enjoyed during the eighties. I don't think he had envisioned what would happen when we got to "Sussudio."

Mark had been very organized about all this. There was no question it had been planned. I had always known him to be a planner, or what seemed like a planner, but *what the hell did I know?*

My mother kneels on the padded bench next to the coffin and tugs at the skirt of my black wrap dress as if to say this is what we should do now. My father's side of the family is not the Catholic side, it's the "not religious at all" side, so I hadn't thought to kneel and still don't consider it appropriate. She clasps her hands in prayer and elbows me in the thigh, so I kneel down next to her and do the same.

I'm sorry, Mark, is what I say to myself, and because we're praying, ostensibly his spirit. *I'm sorry. I'm so sorry.* I try to think of more and better things to say, but I am haunted by "Sussudio," and even though I hate it, I sing along quietly in my brain. *What a wretched, wretched song.* My mother dabs the corners of her eyes with a balled up piece of tissue and makes the sign of the cross before standing and walking away. I do the same thing in the same order.

I really do not know the correct thing to feel. I try to recall my memories of Uncle Mark, but they are not terribly plentiful. I remember he once dressed up like Santa Claus and gave out the gifts at the family party on Christmas Eve night. I must have been in preschool or kindergarten at the time.

He wore a plastic Santa mask with large eyeholes, so it was obvious to me that he was not Santa, but I played along, like I played along at catechism, because it made the adults feel good about themselves. Marnie had already told me Santa wasn't real in a fit of pique when I went into her room without permission.

I recall Mark was handsome, with dark brown hair and blue eyes, a striking combination. He coached his sons' sport teams, didn't he? I think he did.

He puked behind the garage last Christmas.

He spent a lot of time at Grandma's house, helping her with things, trimming her trees and mowing her lawn. He was very good at fixing things, people said.

He liked horses?

We were supposed to go to dinner over parents' weekend—and I had lied and said I had to work—and now I will never go to dinner with him again.

I try to recall just one conversation we had, but I can't. We may never have had one, just us two.

I go over to the photo collage and take in clues. I look at cards on the flower arrangements, but I don't know any of the people who sent them. There are many, many arrangements, so many they make a wall. I count them, but I forget the number.

Strangers arrive to pay their condolences. They pack the room, which crowds with sad faces and slumped postures, low voices—funeral voices. People pair up to talk about my uncle.

I eavesdrop. "Why?" I hear a lot. I wonder it myself.

Didn't he know he mattered?

The room gets hot, and I go outside to cool off. There are people out there too, lined up around the corner of the funeral home and down the street, many of them teenaged or young boys. A lot of them have been crying. I wonder if Mark coached them in some kind of sport. *What sport would that be? Isn't hockey a thing here? Lacrosse, maybe?*

I want to ask them who he was, but think better of it.

I don't know much about Mark's suicide, and when I try to ask about the details, people bark at me to be quiet. The details come much later, from my father, who says that Mark sold his belongings and wrote a goodbye letter. He went to Fort Ontario—the historic site where the French fought the English in 1756—and took photos of himself on the grass in the sun. (He's wearing a faded gray sweatshirt and seems quite happy. The grass is sunlit behind him, which is odd, because there's never any sun in Oswego.) He drilled a hole in the wall between his house and garage, and ran a length of tubing from the exhaust pipe of his car through the hole. He must have sold his bed, because he died on a cheap blow-up mattress, and when I think of where he chose to be when he left this world, how cheap it was, and how he must have thought there should be an easy way to wrap his body up and toss it in the trash like a moldy block of cheese gone bad, I feel such sadness inside I can hardly bear it.

He did not know he mattered, *at all*.

When calling hours end, family members and close friends gather for the funeral in the viewing room, and sit in two neatly arranged sections of white leather chairs. My father sits in the front row with his three remaining brothers, and because each section is five chairs wide, there is an unfortunate chair at end of the row that remains empty. It pains us all to see it. *What's the opposite of serendipity?*

My cousin Evan gives a stone-faced eulogy and is clearly in some form of terrible shock. He is followed by Mark's best friend—a short and stocky man of forty, with an edge—whose words are peppered with anger as he tells us Mark was beloved, and Mark was a great man, and losing Mark is a tragedy. He says it as if we need to be convinced of it. He says he's known Mark for decades, and never knew he had four brothers.

At this, my father's back begins to quiver, and I hear him sniffling and snorting. He bends over and sobs into his hands, making great heaving sounds, and it is a bizarre sight. I have only seen my father cry once, during his grandfather's funeral, and that was fifteen years ago.

I wonder if they would have had a funeral for me. Would he have cried?

> YOU DON'T MATTER, ERIN. DON'T COMPARE YOURSELF TO MARK. YOU'RE NOTHING.

My belly starts to burn a little. There's a feeling in there, and it isn't pleasant. It drifts up my chest and I tighten down my throat to keep it in. It must be terrible sadness, I think. The feeling persists, pushing at the knot in my throat.

It's coming out.

Here it is.

But it is not sadness, as I had suspected. It is anger, and with it comes a very foreign-feeling thought:

Maybe I am not the problem here.

☙ ☙ ☙

People mill about after the funeral. Strangers sign the guestbook by the door with a pen on a chain. Arrangements are made for a funeral procession to the family cemetery, where Mark will share a resting place with the mysterious, stern-faced people from the old photo albums in Grandma's den.

I think about my foreign thought, and get angrier. I'm awash in the feeling, and though I know my feelings are wrong, and this one is probably extremely wrong and therefore as selfish as can be, it makes me feel alive somehow. I feel...*powerful?*

Words begin to fill my head for some reason I can't understand. They, too, feel foreign, and there are a lot of them. I have to get them out.

We bury Mark at the family graveyard, maybe the coldest and most windswept place I have ever been outside of Alaska. My family is in great pain as he goes into the ground. The jokes start coming, to keep everyone from crying, I suspect, because they come out of windpipes quivering with emotion.

We hover in the cold by Mark's grave for what feels like an eternity. No one wants to leave him behind.

That night, all bets are off with regard to underage consumption of beer at my grandparents' house. Nobody cares, or everybody is too despondent to pay attention. I play a game with my cousins we call "Ninety-nine Bottles of Beer on the Wall," which is nothing more than drinking as much beer as possible.

When everyone goes to bed, I lie on the sofa in my grandparents' den for hours, completely unable to sleep. My head is full of more foreign thoughts I never considered before, little fires here and there in me at odds with the rest. The house is empty, too hot, and too quiet. I can hear it whisper to me. *Kill yourself*, it says.

But why, asks a little foreign feeling.

Mark smiles down at me from the wall above, from some happy moment in the seventies, his senior picture, I guess. He wears a bulbous crown of hair and thick glasses.

More thoughts come up.

I get up and go to my bag. I pull a notebook and pen from it, and I begin to write things down.

Nothing will ever be the same for me.

Snakes

A recurring dream from childhood

I am hanging from a tree branch, and my grip is beginning to give way. There is a pit of snakes beneath me dug into the earth next to the tree. The snakes slither in and out of horrible balls full of scales and tongues and fangs. Sometimes, they rear up and snap at my toes.

My father is standing at the base of the tree near the trunk. He looks up at me and then down into the snake pit.

"Dad!" I yell to him. "What do I do?"

He says nothing.

The tree branch starts to move under my hands and my grip loosens a little more. I realize with horror that this is not a branch at all. It is a giant snake.

It leans in to get a better look at me, hisses into my face, and then snaps its fangs.

I let go of it and fall into the pit.

The snakes curl over and around me, hissing and snapping. Dad leans over the side of the pit and looks down at me.

"Dad," I yell to him. "Help me!"

He says nothing.

THE BAD ONE

Part

TWO

LOVE

I AM TWENTY-SEVEN YEARS OLD, LIVING IN THE CITY OF CHICAGO WHERE I WORK AS A FREELANCE GRAPHIC DESIGNER.

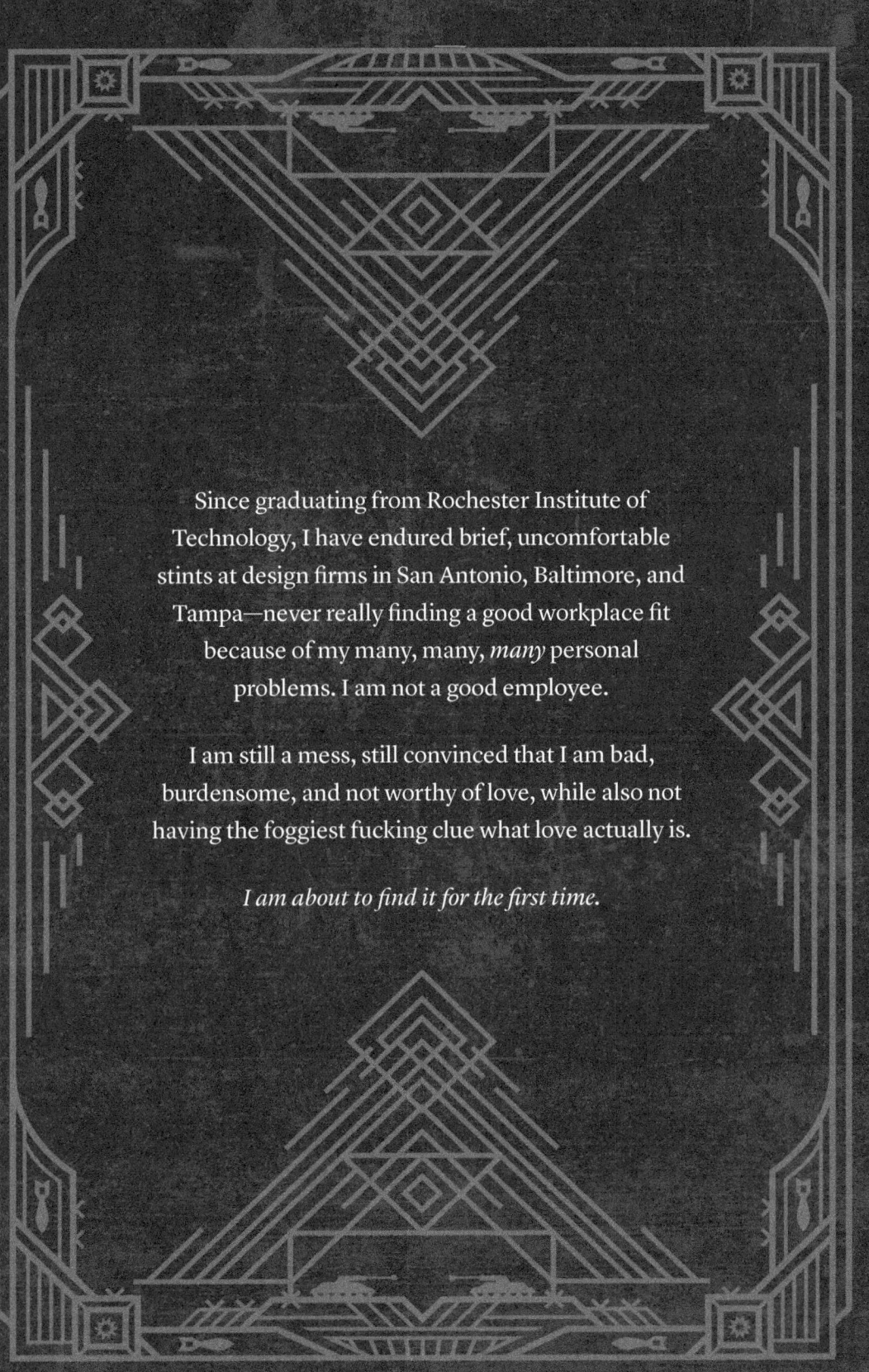

Since graduating from Rochester Institute of Technology, I have endured brief, uncomfortable stints at design firms in San Antonio, Baltimore, and Tampa—never really finding a good workplace fit because of my many, many, *many* personal problems. I am not a good employee.

I am still a mess, still convinced that I am bad, burdensome, and not worthy of love, while also not having the foggiest fucking clue what love actually is.

I am about to find it for the first time.

I am walking down Montrose Avenue in the cold without a coat, my Chuck Taylors slipping around in brown slush. I have boots and coats, and could have put them on before I left the apartment, but it simply seemed too exhausting to look for them.

Nearly ten years has passed since Mark's death and the night I made the vomit-and-CD-case angel on the floor of my college apartment. I don't get so sad I want to die anymore, but I am still troubled.

I'm on one of my long, head-clearing walks, on which I drink coffee, brood, and contemplate my troubled existence—my head filling with lots of words I'll later write down in order to better understand myself. I go for these walks almost every day. I walk marathons over the course of a week, writing in my head, my teeth chattering in the cold.

I am in another one of my "Erin Type" relationships.

An Erin Type relationship is not recognizable as an actual relationship from an outside perspective. Clinicians wouldn't approve. It isn't the coming together of two fully formed people to form a bond of intimacy under a pleasant umbrella of mutual respect. There is no respect, in fact, and no intimacy—unless a lack of boundaries qualifies as intimacy, which it does not. Erin Type relationships are defined by the "absorption" of one troubled, weaker entity (me) into a more powerful, black-hole-like entity (the other). This other has almost no empathy for me, and often lacks empathy for any and all creatures of nature, let alone those they absorb into their being and use at will to bolster their own aims. If an Erin Type relationship is done correctly, I should feel like absolute dog shit day and night, with the hope that if I do enough for the other tomorrow, I will finally earn their love.

That is my understanding of love—that it is extremely conditional—and you are only rewarded with love if you are perfect enough and make great sacrifices for your loved ones. Also, if you truly love someone, you should hate yourself for their benefit.

Remember when Mary, from the movie *Aliens*, was found by Ripley, nearly dead and half eaten by the Xenomorph hive, a gestating Chest Burster in her torso? Remember when she opened her eyes and groaned, "Please kill me?" Mary was in an Erin Type relationship.

This must appear to be painful from the outside perspective, and also a complete waste of time and energy. I imagine those not in Erin Type relationships wonder why the fuck they are happening, how someone could possibly do that to themselves, and whether or not mental illness is involved, which it isn't. Not on my part, anyway.

Erin Type relationships are recreations. They have a specific purpose that is not obvious to me at twenty-seven in my Chuck Taylors on my cold walk. I know very little about why I seem to "end up" in them, randomly and without any kind of purposeful seeking on my part. I merely think I am cursed. Or I think I am unworthy of love.

But I'm about to alter the trajectory of my life the same way I did the night of Mark's funeral, when I started writing all the new thoughts down.

I stomp into what seems like a small puddle while crossing Paulina Street, but it is, in fact, a large pothole full of icy slush. One of my Chucks falls into the hole and splashes icy goo onto the other one. My jeans, up to my knees, are covered in cold muck, and now I am shivering, cold wrapped around my bones.

I think about turning around and going back to my apartment, but I know there's a convenience store around the corner on Clark. I go there every day for a walk coffee. I hurry there, grab some napkins and wipe the slush off my pants. I fix myself a coffee with hazelnut creamer and pay the old man behind the counter. He smiles and says hello. "Out for a walk again?" he asks.

"Yes," I say.

I take gulps of the coffee to warm up as I walk, though it's still too hot and burns my mouth and throat. I stomp down the street and think of a new story and how I will word it.

I write full stories now, stories that begin with odd fixations that seem to arise out of nowhere—just like the Erin Type relationships—and spin my brain into fits, never dropping them until I pass out from alcohol or exhaustion or the writing gets done. Even then, I pick the story back up and I write it and rewrite it. I am obsessed with the stories.

I post my stories on a blog called the "Bunny Blog." People read it and have binary reactions to it. Some love it, and some hate it. Some say "you're crazy," and call me ugly and say they would never have sex with me, as if I'm not acutely aware I'm one of those thick-waisted, small-breasted ladies nobody goes crazy for. The others say I write things they think or feel but don't feel free to talk about.

Sometimes they write me and ask, "Why do you hate yourself?" and I know it is because they hate themselves too and hope I can give them some insight. I don't have any insight to give, and that's the whole point of the writing exercise, to find some. I hope to someday give them an answer, which is—ironically—closer than ever before, in a mere three-block walk down Ashland Avenue.

I see a flash of somewhat spastic movement behind a shop window to my right. There are two tiny pink things pressed against glass and between them, a wiggly black mess. I walk over to the window to get a closer look.

The paws belong to a black puppy with white, socked feet—a squiggly little baby with a swollen, spotted belly. She licks wildly at the window, and my chest feels light. I touch the window and smile. "Hello, there," I say. It seems to be interested in my finger.

My shins are frozen. It couldn't hurt to go inside and meet this pup properly.

The shop is full of designer breeds, chirping in sad, floor-to-ceiling stacks of cages. I walk over to the window to see my black puppy with the socks. I poke a cold finger through the bars and she licks and chews the end of it, which tickles. The sign on her cage says, "Blue Heeler Mix (F)." I don't know what that is, but I am in love with it.

She chirps and spins in circles, kicking up strips of newspaper underfoot, her tail abnormally long and whipping her in her own snout. I look into her sparkly meatball eyes as she licks the bars, my fingers, the air itself—anything she can get her tongue on, really—and something deep in my soul says:

ERIN, THIS IS YOUR DOG.

"Can I see this one?" I ask the surly lady behind the counter.

She unlocks the cage and swoops the puppy into my arms as if it were a sack of rice. "Don't take off with her," she says on her way back to her chair.

I sit cross-legged in front of the shop in the cold with my black puppy between my legs. I giggle as she jumps, turns spastic circles, and wiggles her hind end. I scoop her up into my arms and she licks my chin, my cheeks, and my ears. I cradle her in the crook of my arm like I would a baby and rub her spotted pink belly, which I have to admit reeks of piss. Her long pink tongue dangles from the side of her mouth.

I think I will call you Murph.

💩 💩 💩

Six months have passed. It is a weeknight, and I am working on a logo at my desk. The work is due to my client in the morning, and I am blocked and struggling to get it done.

Suddenly I notice an odor of vomit. *Where is Murph?*

I had given her a rawhide to chew on and set her under my desk. She had gnawed on the rawhide happily, breaking every so often to lick my foot, and it had seemed like I would get some work done tonight. But now she is not under my desk and I smell vomit and shit.

I get up and head toward the kitchen. It's Murph's favorite place.

⏪

I want to be clear about this, because it is an important part of Murph's character: Murph loves food. *A lot.* And when I assert that my dog, Murph, loves food, I know it seems trite and obvious, but that's only because a normal understanding of dog food lust doesn't really apply to this dog and her relationship with food. This is something different altogether, an insatiable, primal hunger, and an obsession.

The surly bitch from the puppy shop sent me home with deworming pills to give Murph in a bit of pâté, which I balled around each little pill in a sort of liver-based Trojan horse and gave to Murph, who drew blood on three of my fingers trying to get at the pâté. Later that night, she ate a hole in the side of her jumbo bag of kibble, gorged herself, vomited, ate the vomit and then shit three times behind the sofa.

Friends mentioned the swelling in her belly, and asked if I had dewormed her. I would tell them, yes, I had given her the deworming pills, and hadn't seen any evidence of worms in her poop, nor any reduction in belly swelling.

"Don't puppies have pot bellies?" I'd ask, knowing

so little about how to raise one apart from articles I read on the internet.

I took Murph to the vet for a checkup just to be sure, and they too were concerned about her food lust and belly size. They squirted spray cheese onto a wooden stick and held it up for her to lick clean as they grabbed some skin on her tush and injected her with medicine. She barely noticed the needle, and then begged for another cheesy stick with her sparkly meatball eyes, which she got from the lovesick tech with ease.

Once again, there was no evidence of worms, nor any reduction in belly swelling.

The food lust only worsened, and though she was fed perfectly apportioned kibble meals at 8 a.m. and 4 p.m. on the dot—God help me if her kibble was even thirty seconds late—she still ate just about anything not nailed down, both organic and inorganic. She ate grass, acorns, and cigarette butts on walks. She ate her own rubber and plastic toys, and anything she could steal from the trash or recycling bin. She ate the stuffing from her dog bed, the cover of her dog bed, pillows, couch cushions, drywall, wainscoting, art supplies, shoes, and a mini bottle of Elmer's glue. At the dog park, she hoarded tennis balls to tear apart and eat behind trees or under benches, often trotting around with three in her mouth at a time, two in the front and one shoved into the back of her throat. (In Murph's lifetime she will eat: glass, a box of unopened tampons, used tampons, clothing, balls of her own fur after grooming, poop, a desiccated possum carcass, a live frog, a bag of cotton balls, a full bottle of allergy medication, an oil painting, WD-40, furniture, hundreds of yards of dental floss, and three large dark chocolate bars that resulted in an overnight stay at the ER, and one 900-dollar fart.)

A friend recommends I try a natural deworming treatment, just a few drops of different tinctures made from barks and herbs mixed into her meals. This "did the trick," which is apparently the phrase I use for horrifying experiences, because this time it refers to the two-foot-long roundworm that came out of my two-foot-long puppy, wrapped casually around a log of digested kibble, toy stuffing, and chunks from a rubber ball.

Though the nightmare of the unexplainable hunger is officially over, Murph never really recovers. There will always be an emptiness in her, an existential hole that she will try to fill with food. It's one of the reasons we get along so well.

On my way to the kitchen to find Murph, and the source of the vomit smell, I check behind the sofa. Sure enough, there are several piles of shit behind it. Half of this mission's objectives are achieved! I wipe the little piles up with a roll from the bulk pack of paper towels I keep next to the sofa, for this very reason, and then I mop the floor with the mop and bucket full of bleached water I fill every morning and set in the living room so that I have easy access to a means of cleaning up the eventual excretory surprises of the day.

It's important to note that Murph has many fears and that these fears are pretty irrational, and exaggerated in scope.

This is my fault, surely. Murph is still a young pup and therefore an emotional sponge. Every neurotic thought within me—and all my incorrect emotions—travel right down the leash into Murph's little body and brain, and they infect her with fear, which has an unfortunate effect on her bladder, so that when she is anxious or frightened, when she hears any kind of loud noise—a doorbell, the heat kicking on in my old building, a neighbor walking by in the hall, or even a car backfiring two streets away—she locks up, squats, and a nervous stream of pee comes whooshing out of her.

Often, she has difficulty peeing or pooping outside, because of all the scary sights and noises—the horrible roars of diesel engines, those contraptions with the ball bearings that make people move too fast, such as skateboards or scooters, any kind of crutch-like devices that disabled people use, hats and long beards, children's light-up wheelie sneakers, rough winds blowing branches to the ground, the clanging of the metal gates, geese of any kind doing anything, automated car washes, and plastic bags. She especially hates plastic bags, and if the wind picks up and the bag begins to float and move, Murph squeals, falls onto her back and pisses all over her own belly.

But the thing that Murph hates the most? *Nail clippers.*

I begin each nail-trimming session with a walk around the block in effort to empty her bladder as much as possible. I take off all my clothes and clear the living room floor of any non-waterproof items. I give her several treats to put her in a calm state, gently patting her head while she eats them. I tell her what a good girl she is, in soothing tones. When she's done snacking, I slowly introduce the clippers to her, letting her sniff them. At this point, she usually starts to pee. I don't know how, but it seems like there is always pee inside Murph, ready to come out.

Time is of the essence now. I dip down for a pretend hug, scooping her into my arms and gently laying her on her side. When I snip the first of her dewclaws, she lets the pee fly, and by the time I'm done snipping the second one, she usually dips her tail—out of nervous wagging—into the puddle beneath her, and flings piss this way and that about the living room, onto her own body and all over me.

💩 💩 💩

Solutions. That's what you look for, right? When it's your dog, and you would do anything for her—and she pisses in fear eight times a day—you roll with the punches and figure out a solution, right? That's what we did, me and my Murph.

A friend gives me the idea for the diapers. They make them for adult female dogs in heat, but can be used for the purpose of training dogs with nervous wetting issues to be more confident. The theory is, if the dog makes a nervous wet, their owner is distressed by it, and though the dog has no idea what they've done wrong, they pick up on the negative energy and become upset and insecure. By catching the mistake, the diapers create an opportunity for the dog to become more secure.

Also, they look a bit like doggy hot pants made of denim, and there's an adorable hole in the seat of them for your dog's tail. I keep Murph in them all day and night, changing them whenever she has an accident, and they are effective almost immediately.

Murph seems more confident, even proud of herself, and it brings tears to my eyes.

💩 💩 💩

I swoosh the mop through the dirty water in the bucket, pull it out again and pull the ringer to get the water out of it. I set the mop on the floor and lean the handle against the wall. The shit smell is mostly taken care of, but the vomit smell is still quite strong.

"Mur-phy" I sing, exaggerating the syllables of her name in a pleasant way. If she thinks I'm mad, she'll scurry off and hide.

She's not in the kitchen, curiously. I often find her here taking running leaps at the trashcan to tip it over and feast on scraps. I once found her here with her head stuck in a jumbo-sized jar of peanut butter I bought from the bulk store, and ever since then, I've been careful to rinse my recycling. I check the bin, but it seems as full as it was yesterday, and the trash is unmolested. Suspiciously, the cabinet under the sink is open, and on the floor beneath it lays an empty bulk bag of sushi rice, a few stray grains, and one half-eaten dish sponge.

Where the hell is she?

The vomit smell intensifies as I walk to my bedroom, and when I flip on the light, I see Murph lounging in the middle of my bed astride a large glob of vomited sushi rice (and half a sponge, I guess), looking sedated and content. Her eyes, half closed from the pleasure of fullness, seem to say she approved of the meal.

Goddamn it, Murph.

I pick her up and take her to the bathtub. She becomes quite nervous as I begin to run some warm water. She licks my forearm out of anxiety, her ears nervously pinned back. I scoop water onto her thick black fur.

"Yes, I know it was tasty," I say to her, trying to calm myself down. *How many gluttonous binges have I had in that very bed?* How could I judge?

"Yes, I know, Murph. It was delicious."

I rub oatmeal-scented soap into her fur—over her tush, down her tail, and into the thick mane around her neck. She seems to like that quite a bit. She slaps her socked paws into the water, and bites at the splashes she makes. At one point, she slips and falls onto her side, squealing a little, and I right her again. I wrap her up in her piggy towel and hold her in my arms for a spell. I set her down and dry her wriggling body off.

People tell me to get rid of Murph. They say she's too much, too food-crazed, and she pees everywhere.

I can't explain why, but with every chirp and squiggle and lick to the nose from this sweet little being, I feel fuller somehow. I really don't know what to call this strange and wonderful fullness, but I know I can't live without it.

It's a hot summer night. Mom and Dad have taken us to the drive-in to see my first movie, *E.T. the Extra-Terrestrial*, a story about a special relationship between a boy and his alien friend.

I didn't just like this movie; I *fell* into this movie. I became this movie. I was Elliott and E.T.'s third buddy—a second Drew Barrymore. I was there with Elliot, creating a careful trail of Reese's Pieces to coax E.T. inside so we could all be best friends for life. I hid E.T. in the pile of toys and pedaled my bike through the sky. I crossed the moon while onlookers gawked and thunderous music rang out into the heavens.

You cannot convince me I *didn't*.

And when E.T. went home to be with his own kind, leaving us all behind for the rest of eternity—though necessary for his own survival—I died inside.

No, I died. I'm dead. I'm not going to make it.

So I am bawling in the back seat of the family station wagon. Snot is draining down my upper lip into my mouth.

"It's okay, honey," says Mom, patting my knee from the front seat. I kick the back of her seat with my sport sandals.

"IT'S NOT OKAY!" I sob to her, breathless. "HE'S GONE!"

Mom rubs my knee and tells me it's just a movie, and that it's silly to be so upset about a movie, but it doesn't feel like "just a movie" to me. No, it feels horribly real, as if Steven Spielberg has drilled down into some part of me nobody was ever supposed to tap.

Marnie is annoyed. "Stahp," she says. "Why won't she stop, Mom?"

Mom shushes her and rubs my leg some more. I sob on.

I'm dying. I'm dead.

E.T. flew off in the end. He said goodbye to Elliott and he just flew away. They will never see each other again. E.T. took his love away. Elliott had love and then, whoosh, it was gone forever.

This thought haunted me in my bones, because I couldn't explain it and yet I knew I was already deeply well-acquainted with it: there could be love, and it could be taken away from you—and no matter what you do, no matter how good you are, or how hard you work, or how many hurdles you jump over—it will never come back to you.

YOU HAVE NO CONTROL.

Of course, I am just a baby, so I can only hurt and cry, which is precisely what I do. Tears stream down my face and neck. My guts are hot with big feelings I can't put words to, feelings that don't have edges or boundaries or names or parameters. I'm a boiling stew of raw, unwelcome emotion.

Mom and Dad take us out for ice cream. I eat it and sniffle.

MURDER
SHE WROTE

SUMMER OF '82 — OSWEGO, NY

I try to swallow, but it's like there are a thousand pins-stuck in my throat. My face and neck and whole body feel hot. I don't understand what's happening to me, and I think I might die. Also, *where is Daddy?*

I don't know what a "sy-nus" is, and I don't know why mine are infected. As I grow, I'll become well acquainted with them, but this is my first infection, so I don't know that when the seasons change, my head will fill up with goo, and though it feels like it will pop, it won't. I will be fine.

Mom comes to the couch and tries to comfort me. She makes me take a little cup full of delicious, orange-flavored medicine I can't enjoy because of the needles in my throat.

"It hurts," I tell her. She says she knows. "Where's Dad?" I ask, and she says he's coming home soon. She puts a washcloth on my forehead and some mentholated goo on my chest to help me breathe, before going back to dinner with Marnie in the kitchen.

Dad is in the woods again, the stupid, STUPID woods.

It's a feeling I feel too often, a desperate need for Dad. If you crack me in two, you'll see that I am hollow. Those golden moments I've captured Dad's attention, when he looks at me, speaks to me, and then I am there—full, gloriously full and real—they are not enough in number, and I need more.

The medicine does its work and I fall to sleep on the sofa. When I wake, I am being hoisted into Dad's arms as he carries me to the car in my jammies. He buckles me into the back seat and Marnie climbs in next to me, excited about something.

It's a hot summer evening, and I roll down my window so the wind cools my face. I can see shiny puddles in the distance on the road, "mirages," Dad says, just a trick of the heat on your eyes.

I ask Mom where we are going, and she says we're going to the Oswego Speedway to watch the races, but I will be staying with Grandma at her house, because I am sick.

I wonder why my Grandma Phyllis—my mother's mother who lives many miles away in Baldwinsville, and is the only real grandparent in my life—would be in Oswego?

When we pull into the farmhouse driveway—the home of my paternal grandmother—I become nervous and ask my mother where Grandma Phyllis is. She laughs a little and tells me Grandma Tyler will watch me tonight, everything will be fine, and that I should be a good girl.

Dad scoops me up and carries me inside while my mother and sister wait in the car, and I cling to him monkey-like and dig my nails into his back.

Please don't leave me here.

I push my face into Dad's shirt as Grandma greets us in the dining room. I can hear her voice on my back. She tells Dad to put me on the sofa in the living room, the mint brocade sofa. He lays me down and I roll toward the cushions. He covers me with an afghan and tells me to be good. I shake my head, yes.

I hear the family car pull out of the driveway and accelerate up the hill toward the speedway. I can hear the cars zoom around the track as they run warm-up laps. I want to go there too. I want to eat cotton candy and cheer on Uncle Mark in his pit crew suit, while he changes the big black tires very fast with a special tool.

Grandma goes into the kitchen. I hear her open a cabinet and then turn on the faucet to fill up a glass. I hear her light-as-a-feather footsteps fall in the dining room, and come closer until I can feel her hovering over me now.

I close my eyes and pretend I'm asleep. I hold my breath.

She sets the glass down on the coffee table, probably on one of her *National Geographic* magazines.

I hear the grandfather clock ticking, and feel my heart beat in my head.

She walks back to the kitchen.

I count the stitches in the brocade flowers on the cushion, running my fingers over the fibers, staying still so she doesn't come back.

The clock ticks. Time passes. I count.

The cars are racing at full speed now. I can hear them zooming around the track, and I can hear the crowd cheer. I imagine I am there, next to Dad, a big blue puff of spun sugar in my hand. The cars zoom around our corner and he tells me some factoid or tidbit about cars I don't understand or care about, but I grin like mad because he's looking at me, and talks to me now and it is magic.

I hear the squeak of a chair in the kitchen and the sound of Grandma's slippered feet coming back now. I close my eyes again and hold my breath as she turns the television on and flips to a certain channel. She sits down in her easy chair in the corner and puts her feet on the ottoman. She rocks back and forth in her recliner.

Squeak, squeak. Squeak, squeak.

I count the threads. Three hundred and thirty three. Three hundred and thirty four. I try to keep my midsection very small and still, taking the air in ever so slowly so she doesn't come over.

We watch three episodes of *Murder, She Wrote* like this.

Then the cars aren't roaring anymore, and I hear our car pull into the driveway. Dad comes inside and scoops me up. I cling monkey-like to his torso as he thanks Grandma for watching me.

I don't open my eyes until we pull out of the driveway.

It's difficult for me to tell this story. My Grandma Phyllis was a good lady. We spent a lot of time together when I was a kid, and though she was a bit bonkers and often told me I was bad, she was also a loving grandmother who really tried to be in my life. I don't think I appreciated her enough.

She was honest with me in ways adults never were, and we had great conversations about things nobody else would talk to me about. I used to beg to go spend the night with her at her seniors' apartment, play dominoes, eat bowls of ice cream, and watch Syracuse basketball games.

She once took me on a trip to Niagara Falls. We went sightseeing, saw the orcas and dolphins at SeaWorld, and she paid a man to airbrush my name onto a unicorn tee that had sexy shreds and beads on it. I thought it was the most excellent tee ever.

This particular weekend trip to Grandma Phyllis's might have been the only time during my childhood that she offered me a taste of what it was like to be my mother.

⏪

I'm setting up my sleeping bag on the living room floor of Grandma Phyllis's apartment in the space of carpet between her davenport and television.

Grandma doesn't like me to sit on the pink davenport. (That was a thing back then. The furniture was for entertaining, and kids were not allowed to sit on it.)

Earlier, Grandma and I had enjoyed the fine French dinner she had cooked us, and though it had been delicious and I had eaten several platefuls, I am hoping I can get my hands on the carton of Neapolitan ice cream Grandma always keeps in her freezer.

"Go ahead," she says, swinging a dishtowel toward the fridge.

I sit on the floor and eat ice cream, while Grandma and I watch *Wheel of Fortune*, her favorite television show. She thinks Pat Sajak is very handsome.

I begin to feel poop cramp in my lower belly, and so I get up and walk toward the bathroom.

"Where are you going?" asks Phyllis.

I tell her I have to poop.

"I don't think you do," she says. "I think you should sit back down."

This sort of thing has happened before in the past, but never with poop. Often, I'll spend the night at Grandma's and she won't allow me to do anything but brush my teeth in the bathroom. I am to touch nothing, and if I do touch things, I am to wipe them down.

Phyllis is a bit weird about toilets in general. If we go places together, she will not allow me to use the public restrooms, because she's frightened that people from a far away place she calls "Sandinistas" are spreading diseases—like the flu, or something she calls "the clap," or even the AIDS virus—

via restroom toilet seats.

I do as Grandma says, and sit back down. There is still ice cream in my bowl, but my midsection is too preoccupied with other concerns for me to want to finish it.

I dump the ice cream, wash my bowl, and set it on the drying rack. Then I get into my sleeping bag and Grandma turns out the lights and wishes me a goodnight.

▲ ▲ ▲

The next morning after toast I ask Grandma if I may shower, and she says I may not. I protest and sass her a little, but she says I will catch my death of pneumonia if I get my head wet. She's seen it before and she knows it will happen again.

I tell her it is the middle of July, and that sort of thing only happens in winter.

She says I may not shower, but I can brush my teeth.

Around mid-morning, I ask her if I can use the restroom.

"Number one or number two?" she asks. I tell her it is both. "You can go number one if you want, but you better not go number two."

I spend a trying day drawing pictures on the floor, and groaning every so often as I squeeze my butthole as hard as I can to keep from pooping my pants.

That night I sneak to the bathroom when I think Grandma Phyllis is asleep. The bathroom door hinges squeak as I pull it shut.

"What are you doing?" calls Phyllis, from her bed.

"Nothing," I say. I get back into my sleeping bag.

▲ ▲ ▲

Around nine o'clock the next morning, as Phyllis is drinking her coffee and I'm attempting to eat a bowl of Mini-Wheats, the pressure inside me becomes unbearable, and I know that if I do not go to the bathroom, I will mess myself. I tell my Grandma, and she becomes very anxious.

"I think it's time for you to go play outside," she says, pointing toward the empty courtyard of her seniors' assisted living complex, where there are a few trees and benches, but nothing else.

Phyllis stands over me as I put my shoes on and climb down her stairwell. I limp out the door, into the courtyard and find a tiny bit of privacy behind a water heater. Then I drop my shorts and poop, and it would have been one of the most glorious craps I've ever taken had Grandma Phyllis's downstairs neighbor not walked around the corner with his groceries at that moment.

He grabs my arm in and marches me to Phyllis's door, and she seems truly appalled by my behavior. She marches me up the stairs again and tells me I'm an animal. I hide under the kitchen table as she calls my parents to come get me.

"She did what!" I hear my mother scream on the other end of the phone line.

Dad drives to Grandma's apartment with the shovel he uses to clean up after our Labrador Retriever. He takes care of the poop and drives me home again. On the ride, he asks me why my hair is greasy, and why I pooped in the courtyard. I tell him the truth, and he says "don't lie."

He sighs.

SPACKLES Up The HOLES You Punch In The WALL

LOOKS DARLING In The FAMILY PHOTOS — SAY CHS

SHE COOKS! AND SHE CLEANS! WITHOUT COMPLAINT

Are you too drunk and shell-shocked to parent?

Try: **Cindy DOLL**

She's only a girl — COLLEGE ISN'T NECCESSARY

SHE DOESN'T Have HER OWN OPINIONS — SO YOU CAN FILL HER UP WITH YOURS!

PROJECT ALL of YOUR Faults ONTO HER AND FEEL SUPERIOR By Comparison

YOU'LL NEVER HAVE TO Say I LOVE YOU Again!

"You're not doing it right," says Mom. "You have to rub harder."

I am rubbing as hard as I can in circles again and again. The coffee table squeaks under the old pair of undies Mom uses as a dustrag.

Everything smells lemony.

I stand up and put all my weight into the heels of my hands, and I am a very strong girl, so I know this will do the trick, and I will make the coffee table shine.

"No, no," says Mom. "You're not rubbing it in hard enough."

"I'm rubbing as hard as I can," I say, hands on my hips now—maybe a bit too sassy. I can see my reflection in the sheen.

"Gimme that," says Mom, holding her hand out for the rag.

I give it to her, and watch as she kneels down and sprays the table with a lemony mist and begins to grind the dustrag into the finish in a dizzying succession of circular swipes.

Like with Dad, I go back in time to Mom's childhood a lot, but not for the same reason. With Dad, I go back so I can feel close to him. With Mom, I go back to get distance and clarity.

Feeling close to mom has never been difficult. What's difficult is not feeling so very terribly, horrifically close to, wound around, entwined with, and all around choked to near death. Sometimes I don't know where I stop and she begins, and if

I go back—and I try to understand where she comes from, and why she spins—it is only to grab on to something steady. It is to put up a wall between us two that I can lean on, let the dizzies subside and say, "This over here is Erin, but that over there is Mom."

I imagine it is fifty-seven or fifty-eight. Back then it's just Mom and Uncle JK—many years before Aunt Robyn would be born and solidify Mom's status as middle child, and therefore the most forgettable of the three. Mom can do no right, but Uncle JK can do no wrong, what with his male genitalia, golden-colored brush cut, and pale blue eyes. He's out playing with his buddies, and Mom is inside again, cleaning again.

She's *always* cleaning. ("She was like a slave," says Aunt Robyn of Mom's childhood. "It was *sad*.")

The television is on, and it plays some wholesome fifties type show in black and white about the hero always being heroic and the villain always being villainous. These are black and white times.

Grandpa James is a sherriff, and they live in Syracuse in a boxy little middle-class home, on a street full of similar families who live in identical homes, save for the exterior paint jobs. When he isn't working, he is either drunk or gambling—sometimes both—and when the school bus pulls up out front to drop Mom (and her bloody knuckles) off from another day at Catholic school, it's not uncommon for her and her classmates to see Phyllis's bare ass-cheeks pressed against the bay window, as Phyllis is often shit-canned on gin by four o'clock in the afternoon, which in her defense is truly the *worst* fucking hour.

What is Phyllis doing? Drinking, surely. She must have a drink on her, and it must be a liquor drink in a crystal glass, like the many crystal glasses I have seen on shelves in Phyllis's pretty apartment. She must be foxy. Phyllis is a striking lady, with elegantly styled platinum-colored hair and ruby red nails filed to perfect points and glossed to high heaven.

You've never seen photo albums like theirs. What a looker of a family, with Phyllis in all her hourglass-shaped glory and Mom in her smart dresses, wool suit sets, ribbons, blonde bob, and emotionally vacant but doll-like face.

Maybe Phyllis inspects Mom's work as she cleans. Maybe she hovers over her, raises her eyebrow in judgment, and says, "You're not rubbing hard enough, Cindy." I know someone must have said this to my mother.

In fact, if anything at all is said to my mother—and I believe this is said or implied or suggested on an almost daily basis—it is: *you are not enough, Cindy.* She is not enough of anything. She doesn't try hard enough. She's not good enough, pretty enough, or smart enough.

I believe the eye of my mother's storm is a gigantic flashing neon sign in hot pink and electric blue that says, "You are not good enough, Cindy."

Now Grandpa James is home, having lost his paycheck betting on the horses again. He doesn't acknowledge Mom in the living room as he stomps through the house to the fridge, cracks open a beer—the last thing he needs—and takes big grimacing swigs of it as Phyllis begins to light into him with the questions. How will they pay the mortgage? How will they eat? Why does he do this?

Mom buffs her table in circular swipes, hearing it all, but pretending she doesn't. Does she hear it? If she can get this table shiny enough—shiny enough to see her reflection—things will be better. If she gets the table perfect, everything will be fine. Everything will hover here in fifty-seven or fifty-eight. Everything will pause into a pretty, pretty snapshot of a wholesome black and white family, well-dressed, coiffed and glossed to high heaven.

You couldn't imagine the lengths my amazing, inventive mother has gone to in order to stay in this moment, the spinning and the spinning and more spinning, for years. For decades! For a liftetime, to clean this family up, to see it always from this vantage point. Her loyalty would astound you as much as it would break your heart.

Phyllis and James hurl insults back and forth—the cubes rattling around Phyllis's glass, the beer splashing over the lip of James's can. Mom buffs the table. James finishes his beer in a big, burning glug, and crushes it into a ball before launching it against the wall or the floor—or straight up his ass for all I really know. Mom buffs the table. Phyllis asks James "Who's going to clean that up!" but we all know exactly who will do it. James turns and busts the wall open with the same nasty right straight he once threw at a nun in the heat of his youth, the same right straight he got kicked out of college for. Incidentally, this was a fortuitous right straight. It made him eligible for the draft, and he was sent to the South Pacific, where he fought at the Battle of Okinawa, got shot, won the Purple Heart, held his best friend in his arms as he bled to death, and embarked on a lifelong battle with shell shock he was never really able to drink into submission. Is "lifelong" a term that applies to people who die at fifty-four?

Pieces of plaster crumble to the floor, and James stomps out the door again. Phyllis refills her drink and takes it to the bedroom. Does she cry? I never saw Phyllis cry, and I can't imagine such a thing. In fact, the only emotion I can imagine Phyllis having is paranoia, and I'm pretty sure that's not an emotion. It seems more like a symptom, probably of some crippling mental illness Phyllis never got proper medical treatment for.

Mom squirts more wax onto the table and sets the can on the carpet. She runs the dustrag through the wax in circles, even harder now, as a sniffling Grandma Phyllis goes to the garage for the spackle. I ache to be there with her, next to her on my knees with my own rag. I want to tell her how perfect the table looks—and that her heart is pure and she deserves better than this—but fifty-seven came and went long before there was a me.

It is a warm fall night in 1982. I am sleeping in my bedroom.

I wake to a pounding sound in the hallway and the snap of distant light switches being flicked. I hear the hinges of the door to my sister's bedroom squeal, and the "thwap" of her light switch too. I hear Mom say, "Wake up!" She does not say it quietly. Something is very wrong.

It is dark in my own bedroom. The only light in it is the thin blue sliver from the streetlight that sneaks between my shade and molding. It isn't nighttime, but it isn't daytime, either.

My cat groans and stands up on her socked paws, stretching her back into an arch.

Mom bursts through my door and snaps on my light too. I shut my eyes and rub them with my fists. Mom whips my blanket to the foot of the bed, and I feel the cold air of my bedroom on my legs and belly.

"You're late for school!" she yells. She smells like bleach.

I'm very confused.

Mom goes to my dresser and pulls out some clothes, a shirt, socks, and some undies. She pulls out a pair of corduroy pants and holds them up, pondering the visuals with a cocked hip. What is she thinking? *That this isn't the right pair? I should wear the tan cords with the tee that has the ruffles on the sleeves?*

She tosses the pants next to the shirt, socks, and undies and examines their tones together. Brown and purple must be a big no, because she turns and tears back through the drawer for a different top. What is she thinking now? *Where is the top with the red trimming on the arms and the neck?* Of course I do not remember the details of dressing on this specific morning at five years of age. I merely extrapolate from what I know of Mom, the many mornings she has styled me, and the many, many hours I'll go on to spend with professional photographers, guessing and then second-guessing wardrobe choices in efforts to compose a *perfect* image.

This I remember well: Mom looks frazzled.

Little snakes of her goldenrod-colored hair have fallen from her nighttime curlers. Her skin is shiny with a glaze of sweat and her expression is one I'll get to know very well in the coming years, which is one of paranoid blankness. She's not angry or sad. She isn't anything you could call an emotion unless paranoia is an emotion. Is it? I don't really know. Her eyes are wide and bulging from some kind of swelling behind them, and her irises are tiny green islands in an ocean of bloodshot panic.

Even today, I am torn in two when I see this face. I want to soothe her, but I'm afraid to get too close. *How does one hug a rabid dog?*

She tosses the top with the red trimming onto my bed. "Get dressed," she says, pounding from the room.

I take off my PJs and get dressed. I probably do not put the undies on. In fact, I probably toss them behind my bed because I don't like undies. Too constricting.

I tug my shade to lift it and look out at the street.

Is there a field trip today? There must be a field trip. Will there be chocolate milk?

Mom whips about the house in her nightgown and open bathrobe, wild and unkempt. She can't find her keys and we have to leave now. I find it difficult to believe Mom is going to leave our house like this and go out into the world looking a mess. Mom never leaves our house—even to go jogging with Dad—without fixing her hair and makeup, and making sure her clothes and shoes are just right. She is the prettiest, blondest, and most perfect lady in town, and the very best mother. When we go places together, people always say, "you have the prettiest mom" and I feel so proud. She's the president of the PTA and she organizes all the fundraising events, the school carnivals and cakewalks, and Santa's Secret Shop in November. Most moms bring junk food to snack days, but my mom brings healthy snacks to school—raisins and celery sticks with peanut butter on them. She bakes me birthday cakes in the shape of my favorite Sesame Street characters and sews me dance recital tutus made of satin with sequins on them. She waits in lines outside stores for hours to buy us Cabbage Patch dolls I know we cannot afford. She cooks, and cleans, and washes, and dries, and folds, and wipes, and scrubs—sometimes on her hands and knees, and sometimes furiously, and sometimes with bleach-covered cotton swabs in the tight corners between the linoleum and the molding until she sweats buckets and everything is perfectly clean. Sometimes I don't know why she does this, because there isn't much in the way of dirt there, but Mom sees it. Sometimes it seems she doesn't sit down for days and sometimes Dad calls her "The Whirling Dervish" as she vacuums the living room carpet in mad circles, zooming the vacuum out and in, this way and that, possessed by something none of us can see or hear—something that tells her bad things about herself.

She dresses in smart tops and skirts, and wears gray suede high-heeled boots in the fall. She has goldenrod-colored hair that falls in thick sweeps of waves she keeps in place with aerosol sprays and such, the sides of it feathered like Farrah Fawcett on *Charlie's Angels*, if Farrah Fawcett were a hundred times prettier!

Last summer, the city finally fixed the cracked sidewalk in

front of our house and a neighbor boy wrote, "I heart Mrs. Tyler" in the wet cement, which ticked Dad off to no end.

My sister and I go to the mudroom to put our shoes on. Marnie's hair is in two disheveled pigtails. I ask her what is happening, and she shrugs but says nothing. Mom goes to the pantry and looks around. She comes out with four mini boxes of raisins and hands two of them to each of us. I put mine in my backpack, and watch in shock as Mom splits and tugs on each of Marnie's messy pigtails to tighten them up. As careful as Mom is with her own hair, she is doubly so with Marnie's. Their shared passion for perfect hair and their daily hairstyling love-fest makes me want to vomit from envy.

We climb into the back seat of our old green car, which putts and spurts as Mom turns the key, slams it into reverse, and backs out of the driveway, casting stones into the street. She yanks the gearshift into drive and takes off down the street, the old green car growling as it accelerates. When she pulls up to the front stoop of Phillips Street Elementary this whole ordeal becomes even more confusing. There is no one at Phillips Street Elementary—there are no lights on outside of it, nor are there any inside of it, either. There are no children in the schoolyard and no cars in the parking lot.

"Okay girls," says Mom. "Have a good day."

I look at Marnie. *Do we get out?* She doesn't seem to know what to do, either.

"Girls, go!" says Mom. "You're late."

Marnie yanks on the handle of the old green car and pushes

the door open with her sneakers. It yowls a little from rust. She climbs off the ripped leather seat, and I slide over and climb out too.

"I love you," says Mom through the open back door. I give it a push, it yowls shut, and then Mom takes off down the street and grumbles around the corner. A streetlight buzzes.

Marnie starts to walk to the front door of the school, and I follow her. The door is open, so we go inside. The front hallway is dark, as is the principal's office, the nurse's office, and the rest of the rooms on the floor.

Marnie tells me she's going to her classroom now, and I should go to mine. She turns right and heads around the corner, and then I'm alone.

I go to my kindergarten classroom but there is no one there. I walk from room to room around the school trying to figure out what's going on.

Did they leave for the field trip already? They give us chocolate milk when we go on field trips, and I am not going to get any. We never get it at home because it's bad for you.

I eventually find Marnie in the gymnasium. "Was there a field trip?" I ask. She shrugs.

"I dunno," she says.

We walk back to the front stoop where Mom dropped us off. Marnie sits down on the curb with her arms around her knees, and I sit down too. I play peek-a-boo with a dried leaf and the Kermit on my right Kermit the Frog corrective sneaker that

Mom and Dad just bought for me to fix my bum feet.

Marnie looks sad. I pull one of her messy pigtails. She emits a little squeal—annoyance—and flips the tail back over her shoulder and out of reach. Of course I don't recall if she specifically did this while we sat on the stoop on that very morning when I was five years of age, I merely assume from the many decades of hearing annoyed squeals and their equivalents, always hoping it would go differently.

We sit like that for a period of time, and then we hear the grumbling of the old green car again. It turns the corner and hurls toward us, screeching to a halt by the stoop. Mom furiously rolls down the manual window of the green car and sticks her unkempt head out of it.

"Get back in the car, girls," says Mom. "It's too early for school!"

This will not come as much of a shock, but it is Christmas day and I am very drunk again. If you could go back in time and tap me on the shoulder as I sit on an overturned bucket chugging bourbon in the dark like a ghoul in my father's basement, and ask me why I am doing such a thing, I'll tell you it's because I haven't a clue, or because I am bad and burdensome, or because the beams above me hold the heft of thousands of dollars' worth of gifts my long-suffering family have bought me because they love me and love means buying stuff for people.

Of course, I don't think I've been sober on Christmas since high school.

It's a Christmas *Catch-22*—I couldn't possibly go upstairs and flit about the house with this Bourbon bottle, be honest for once, and say "yes, I am drinking"— and yet I could not possibly stand being here in this house at all today without the sweet numbness that drinking provides.

It is god-awful cold in the basement, and it smells like earth and cat shit from the litter box under the stairs. All I can see of my parents' feral cat, Sybill, are two little eyeballs, staring at me from the dark. She won't come out of her corner until nighttime, and then she'll be brazen and she'll coo for kitty treats or slap Murph around with her little yellow paws, till Murph squeals, jumps into my lap, and pisses into her diaper.

There's a fire popping in the wood stove in the corner, but it does nothing to reduce the chill in my bones. I can make out the faint outline of my dad's workshop table through beams and clotheslines, and the many cobwebs between. It's littered with rusty old tools he inherited from Grandpa after he died, little bits of metal and wood he tinkers with but never really "makes" things with, and all the raw materials you could ask for to both tie flies and make bullets. There are oils, and nuts, and bolts, and guns. There are saws, and screws, and metal boxes full of ratchets. Lord knows what he does with them.

I used to come down here to steal time with him. Sometimes he'd humor me and we'd tie a fly, and I would see his energy drain, and a kind of emotional nictitating membrane close over him and I'd know it would be time to leave. If I stayed too long, he'd get uncomfortable. If I talked about my feelings, he'd sigh and say I was selfish for feeling feelings at all. You don't feel your feelings if you love your family. If I talked about Mom and how mean she was—and how she might have needed help—he'd tell me I should be ashamed of myself because Mom does all our laundry, and I would go back upstairs, sneak three Hostess cakes into my cheeks in the mudroom (for the guilt) and go watch television with my mother and sister.

When I got older I'd come down here to throw up in the overturned bucket I'm sitting on. *How many times had I emptied my innards down here?* Sometimes I think that long after I am dead and gone, a part of me will linger on and haunt this basement. Some poor future soul will come down here to do a wash and see the energy of me, black and slick with abstract rage, like one of those Japanese ghost girls from a horror movie.

I finger the label of the bottle. The graphics could use a punch-up if I'm being honest, because the line work is a little timid, but the printing is expensive—foil stamping and embossing—which is unfortunate, because it means this bourbon is a pricey one. I had hoped to swipe one of the cheaper ones, but then, the cheap ones are hard to find in Dad's cabinet. Dad drinks good shit.

I hear my mother's feet pounding the dining room floor above. She squeaks something to my sister in her nasal, Central New York accent—I can't tell what.

"I don't know where she is," says Marnie.

I wipe my mouth with the sleeve of the brand-new pink cardigan I'm wearing, a Christmas gift from Mom. It's soft, a baby pink color, and would look lovely on her, or on Marnie, or any kind of soft, baby pink kind of woman, but not on me. A little mouth smear of lipstick stains the sleeve of the sweater. Shit. I had forgotten I was wearing it, because I never wear makeup, but part of the "stocking lode" was a pricey lipstick I knew Mom spent a lot of money on to buy me, and I was now wearing it to humor her.

WHAT'S THAT SAYING ABOUT LIPSTICKS AND PIGS?

Family friends are here.

Hello, I say to them, cracking a smile with my perfect-looking shells of inwardly rotted teeth. I'm now a stale kind of drunk, the uncomfortable kind that's gone on too long, and I'm overcompensating to cover it up, careful to both suck in my boiling stomach and pull my perpetually hunching shoulders back. At full pull, when I'm trying my very hardest to be upright, I still look hunched.

So friends are here, and now there is an audience. It's time to tell the story of this perfect family, and time for public relations, or performance, or any other kind of metaphor about families seeming like one thing from the outside looking in, and another thing altogether from within. I never liked these kinds of situations—and I never knew why—and if I felt guilty about that, I merely told myself I was bad, which suits the storyline perfectly. It's *method*.

The first part of the story is that Marnie is *good*.

That's method, too. Marnie is terribly, *undeniably* likable as far as human beings go. She's sweet and considerate. She sends sympathy flowers and gifts for your birthday. She's funny and fashionable. She works a sensible job as a media buyer, earning stuff-buying money by the buttloads and gets to go to the Super Bowl with her equally fashionable coterie of 401(k)-having girlfriends as well as various golf tournaments I don't give a shit about. Dad is always bragging about her perk trips to those tournaments. She has that 401(k) thing everybody talks about, that thing the real grown-up people possess, the magical qualification that opens up the door to the upper echelon of jobness.

She wears funky Boho clothes, has perfectly manicured nails painted blue and green and other up-trend tones, and pays as much per month to maintain her honey-colored, balayaged locks as I spend on rent. Maybe more.

People hug her longer and they squeeze her tighter. They laugh louder at her jokes and ask about her more often. She naturally, without force or provocation, likes what Dad likes. Her thoughts never challenge his, or Mom's either. She never says weird things, like "the Catholic Church is a corporation," or "identity politics are a disease," or "there's something wrong with Grandma." She's smooth to be next to, and has no edges, and there's an ease to the way she walks around this house, as she isn't afraid of anything that may be said to her, as if she is a queen here, untouchable and all around better. There are times I watch her and feel almost sickened with jealousy.

We sit at the dining room table and catch up over pumpkin pie and coffee with sweet liquor in it. Mom's friend, Pat, tells us all about her daughter, who now lives in Maryland, is married, and has three children. I can see my mother's face wince in pain as she hears this.

This is before Facebook, so if you wanted to brag about your grandchildren or married daughter, you carried around an envelope full of photos you could show to people, which is exactly what Pat did. We thumb through them, and Mom emits sad little "aw"s every so often. Adrienne's life with her handsome husband and his good teeth, and her three little boys dressed in matching denim overalls and snappy white button-downs looks perfect. These are perfect pictures. *The truth is probably not so perfect, but then the pictures are good, so what does it matter?* This is the logic.

Adrienne drives an expensive SUV. She lives in a big house with a stone exterior and has a pool and a hot tub. She has blonde highlights—it's so important to have blonde highlights—and takes her boys to Disney World once a year, where they pose in front of that stupid castle you can't go inside wearing black felt mouse ears, grinning from ear to ear the way people who have a lot of stuff always do.

ADRIENNE IS JUST BETTER THAN YOU, ERIN. BUT THEN *EVERYONE* IS.

I smash chunks of pumpkin pie into the roof of my mouth with my tongue. I wash it down with coffee. My jaw is tight with shame and resentment, but I smile through it. I have nothing, and people think my life is worthless because of it.

Pat spends an hour or more talking to Marnie about her life, because Pat likes Marnie. Everyone likes Marnie, actually. Everyone likes the breezy, happy-go-lucky, agreeable, not a care in the world, golden-colored Marnie, with her easy walk and her talents for conversation and most-ever likableness. Oh, she is terribly fucking likable and always has been—even at fifteen, when she sat quietly on the living room floor while Mom styled her very Mom-like hair (blonde highlights), and even at five, when she choked on a corn chip and didn't want to bother anybody so she went off to the living room very quietly to die, and Dad rushed in to save the day and give her the Heimlich. Dad, the hero!

She looks fabulous in baby pink. She doesn't brood in basements drinking liquor straight from bottles.

When they talk about me, what they say is something more along the lines of "Well, you know how Erin is, har har." There's a joke about my weirdness and then nervous laughter, but not real laughter—the kind of laughter you force out because you're nervous your joke isn't funny, and you want the audience to know it's time for them to laugh now.

"It's Erin, har har," they say. They shrug their shoulders. "What can you do?"

Sometimes they talk about me being talented. That seems to be a nice thing adults are willing to say about me after they say I am weird because I am not like them. It's the statement they tack on to the end of the weirdness statement, with a "but" qualifier, like so: "You know, Rich dropped Erin on her head when she was a baby, but she's *so talented*, har har."

Sometimes the family friend will say it. Mom or Dad will say "Crazy Erin, with all that art, har har," and the friend will feel bad for them and say:

"But...she's *so talented*" the way that Dustin Hoffman was *talented* in the movie *Rain Man*.

Sometimes they tell the story about kindergarten parents' night, when my teachers pulled them aside and told them to buy me art supplies, because I wouldn't leave the art corner and eighteen of the twenty randomly selected works they tacked up as a sort of kiddie gallery for parents' night had been mine.

"Eighteen of the twenty!" says Mom.

Sometimes she takes pictures of what I draw and puts them into a little "brag book," she takes around to parties like Pat's envelope.

I can't say for certain that Mom told this story on that Christmas Day. I honestly can't remember the exact conversations we had, but on many Christmas Days when it was a necessary part of the storyline to tell it, Mom did.

I should also say I doubt my mother told this story with such hyperbole, but this is the way I remembered the story, which is why I tell it so. This is how the story locked into my memory, and how it became a tool I could use as both a weapon against myself and a means of forging intimacy with two parents who didn't want to be intimate. If I was their bad one, then I was not *nothing* to them at all.

It's the fourteenth of January 1977, which is the coldest day ever, you should know. It is the beginning of the *Great Blizzard of Seventy-Seven*, and quite literally, there has never been a colder day in the history of humanity. Thermometers explode, and women and children freeze to death in the streets. It is warmer at the bottom of the Marianas Trench than in Upstate New York on this day.

My mother is nine and a half months pregnant with me, and I will not come out, because I'm an asshole. She and my father have been to the hospital two times to have me thus far, which cost them two *co-pays*—and though the doctor had set a deadline for my arrival, I did not show up. Already, I am *unreliable*.

I'm not even supposed to exist, technically. Mom just had Marnie, and she isn't ready to have another baby. There's no plan in place, and no money saved. There had been a boring movie on TV—*David and Goliath*—and nine months later, there's an unreliable baby that won't come out when it should, a promiscuous little egg that skipped its curfew to mingle with the fast sperms in the fallopian tubes, the ones that wear the leather jackets, smoke the cigarettes, and grease their hair back.

The previous trips to the hospital had been on mild days, but now it is the coldest day ever, and I want to come out, probably just to be difficult.

My father warms up the car and helps my mother to it, and then they drive to the hospital in Oswego through record-breaking snowfall. The wind beats the windows of the old green car as their tires slide around in the great, heaping gobs that have fallen in the night. The Great Blizzard of Seventy-Seven is on, and its epicenter is my mother and father's old green car as it drives to the hospital.

There's never been so much snow in any one location in the history of frozen precipitation falling to the ground. There's no more air now, only snow.

My father helps my mother inside the hospital, and it is decided by everyone there—doctors, nurses, janitors even—that I am an asshole baby that cannot be reasoned with, and I am coming out right this instant. Mom is wheeled into a delivery room where she lies on a bed and does her Lamaze breaths—doing her part, and all the things she is supposed to do—but I don't do my part, because my mother's water never breaks.

I am coming, but I am *not* coming, because I am an unreliable jackass of a baby, and when the doctors must manually break my mother's water with a needle, feel free to imagine Janet Leigh and Anthony Perkins in the shower.

I come out with a jet-black Mohawk, and I am surly in the pictures.

My aunts call me "Dream Baby" because I sleep eight hours a night, but Mom never mentions this part, not until many years later.

I looked it up once. The Great Blizzard of Seventy-Seven didn't start until February.

It's ten o'clock, I suppose, though I'm not sure. I know it's late, and the family friends have gone home to plan for another year of excellence and material-good accumulation. My father and sister have gone to bed, and though I wish my mother would do the same, she is still downstairs, sitting across from me at the kitchen table as I neurotically scratch Murph's neck and hover close to the liquor cabinet so I can make moves when the coast is clear.

When stale drunk, one must choose from two equally awful options:

1. SOBER UP, OR
2. PULL THE TRIGGER.

I pulled the trigger.

There is no longer any plausible deniability; I am just drunk, and Mom knows it. What she also knows is that I am poor, difficult, mannish, unmarried, childless, weird, and not attractive in family photos. I am not as good as Adrienne in any way, shape, or form, and that makes her look bad.

What I don't know—but soon will—is that Mom's close friend, Wanda, has a lesbian daughter, and that this daughter recently "came out" of the closet and had what is called a "commitment ceremony" with a longtime girlfriend she met at a prestigious, all-girls college in New England. They had worn matching, tailored white pantsuits and snappy short haircuts with blonde highlights, and the pictures that Wanda showed Mom at Red Lobster Shrimp Fest had been breathtaking. Mom could really see herself as the mother of a lesbian daughter with a snappy short haircut and a white tailored pantsuit. She *really* could. It's a good story.

So Mom leans in and pats my free hand. She tells me that she is "very worried about me."

I cringe, inwardly, because I know it is true she is genuinely concerned for me, but I also know that this statement is a crowbar of sorts, and that this is what Mom uses to pry me open in order to reorganize what's inside of me, and make me more palatable to her social set.

She tells me she is worried about me because of the usual reasons (broke, weird, unmarried, etc.) and that she thinks that I am probably a lesbian. I tell her that I am not a lesbian, but this doesn't seem to be what she wants to hear. We go back and forth like this, for twenty minutes or more, with Mom telling me I am gay and me telling her that I have thought about it quite a bit, and I am quite certain I am not gay.

But who am I to give her notes on her script? She could really see herself as the mother of a lesbian with highlights.

Our disagreement escalates.

"You're gay!" yells mom, red-faced in the doorway to the living room, her nightgown stained with sweat rings around the arms and one baby pink forefinger stabbing at my face. "Just admit you're gay!"

Murph is hiding under my knees, now, her tail thumping, and piss shooting into her diaper.

She turns and stomps out of the kitchen, and I wonder just what in the hell all this was about. It won't make sense to me until many years later, when I sign up for a Facebook account and become friends with Wanda's lovely lesbian daughter, who posts a picture from her wedding every year on the day of her anniversary. She really *can* rock a tailored pantsuit.

By one in the morning, I am on the floor in the living room in a drunken stupor, watching the end of *Emmet Otter's Jug-Band Christmas*, the Jim Henson version of "The Gift of The Magi" acted out by otter puppets—an impoverished mother and son who sacrifice everything they have to buy gifts for each other only to learn that love is the greatest gift of all.

When I think of how these beautiful otters didn't have a pot to piss in, but had love in spades, I am gutted, and I sob into my mother's embroidered duck pillow like an asshole.

I had felt such guilt after my argument with Mom. *Was I gay?*

I could be gay, if that's what she wants. I could get highlights and wear pantsuits.

If I loved her, I should be anything she wants me to be and do everything she tells me to do, and say everything she wants me to say, and like everything she wants me to like until I die.

I look at the pile of Christmas gifts and do some painful math. *How much do I owe this woman? How much do I owe my father— for chrissakes—who worked a job he loathed every day of his life to provide for me?*

I wonder if we could work out a sort of repayment plan, where they tally the total cost of me—all the food and shelter, all the stuff and every co-pay—and I could send them checks every month as installments. Then I can be as weird and fucked up as I want to be.

YOU COULDN'T MAKE THAT MUCH MONEY IN THREE LIFETIMES, LOSER.

I cry harder into the duck pillow, using it as a sort of muffler, so that the gurgles and twisted snort sounds don't travel up the stairs and wake my loved ones. When the crying subsides, I wipe the tears and snot from my face with the sleeve of the cardigan that I have probably ruined during the day's messier moments, the sneaking of brown liquors and such.

I hear a bristling sound by the Christmas tree and turn to see what it is. Murph has been trying to snack on the ornaments all day. I hop up and stumble a little to get around the couch and see what she's up to.

I find Murph by the dining room table in a hunched squat, a log of poop dropping out of the tail hole of her doggy diaper onto my mother's perfectly vacuumed carpeting.

The poop is sparkly with tinsel.

That's a wrap on Christmas, my friends.

My New Career In Otter Love

A PMS NIGHTMARE

EXAMPLE: MOM'S CYCLE, DAY 22

My sister cranks up the volume on the kitchen radio and waves me over to her, excitedly. They're announcing school closings. I stand on my tiptoes, too nervous to be still. "Eek!" I say, crossing my fingers.

The air outside the kitchen window is plump with flakes I inspect for size and speed of float rate, because if they are big, and they float slowly, then this is a phenomenon called "lake-effect snow" and that means the Department of Public Works won't be able to get enough of the city plowed for the busses to make their stops.

Even though the snow falls in great heaps and gobs—and with

greater frequency than it does these days—school was rarely closed. The reasoning for this was the frequency itself; if we closed school every time we had lake-effect snow, school would be out from the end of October to the middle of April. There were times I lost boots in the snowbanks on my walks to school, so deep was the snowfall, and I had to dig down into the bank, yank the boot back out, and put it back on.

And no, the walk to school wasn't uphill both ways.

Mom walks into the kitchen in her robe and slippers and looks out the window. Her peachy nose crinkles as she squints to take in the size and float rate of the flakes. "Oh, girls," she says. "They look pretty fat, don't they?" She pours herself a mug of coffee and waits by the radio with us.

The closure announcements always start in the country and end in the city, where we live, and the schools out in the country are closed quite a bit more often, because it's harder for the plows to cover that much territory in the night.

But they announce that Falconer is closed, and Falconer is just a stone's throw from our school district. Marnie yelps a little, jumps, and then quiets back down. This is a very good sign.

There's a brief panic as they skip our school to announce the closing of the community college.

And then the man on the radio says words from my dreams: "All schools in the Jamestown School District are closed."

IT IS A SNOW DAY!

I jump about the kitchen in my slippers, crashing into the

countertops and knocking things over. Marnie high-fives Mom and we all dance around in the kitchen.

Marnie and I make bowls of cinnamon oatmeal and eat them on the sofa while watching mid-morning television like slugs, waiting for *The Price Is Right* to come on so we can laugh at all the dummies who bid on the first showcase—you never bid on the first showcase, says Mom. My best buddy, Lindsay, shows up at the back door, jubilant in a puffy pink hat, a box of microwave popcorn tucked into her parka. We eat all three bags, shouting out the prices of dish soaps and appliances—and Mom is the best at this, for obvious reasons—and then we paint our nails pink with lighter pink dots, and our fingers look like ladybugs.

Later in the afternoon, we hear the low grumble of a diesel engine outside, and Mom jumps up and goes to the bay window. There's a city truck out front with a plow attached, scooting piles of snow onto the already enormous banks, a thing we often don't see when there is lake-effect snowfall, as we live on a small side street the plowers often skip. We get snowed in a lot, and Mom and Dad get angry.

"Well, I'll be," says Mom.

"Girls, come on" she says as she takes off for the kitchen, pulls out the phone book and runs a nail down the page looking for the number she wants. When she finds it she puts her finger up to her mouth to keep us quiet, picks up the phone, and dials a number.

What are we doing?

We hear the phone line purring out a ringtone and then the click of someone picking up. "Yes," says Mom into the receiver. "Is this the Department of Public Works?"

There's a waa waa noise on the other end, someone at the DPW talking.

"Okay, then," says Mom. "I'd like to report a strange sighting on the streets of our town." Then mom covers her mouth to hold in a burst of laughter. She composes herself a little, and then shouts, "A SNOWPLOW!" into the phone. She busts out laughing and hangs the phone up.

I got my first period when I was eleven, and to me it seemed to ruin my already deteriorating relationships with my family.

Mom had begun a frightening phase in her life during which she had little to no control over her moods, and though it had nothing to do with me, it coincided with the onset of my puberty. It was easy to believe it was my fault, especially since Mom told me it was. By the time I became officially female, Dad decided parenting me wasn't fun for him anymore and he wanted little to do with me. "I liked you when you were a child," he once told me. "But not when you were a teenager." Even at eleven I knew I was standing in the shadow of his mother, but there wasn't much I could do about that, as he was bigger than me and in charge of me, he was my source of food, shelter, and protection, and he was aggressively unwilling to feel things he needed to feel due to some earth-shattering trauma from his childhood that is and always will be a mystery to me.

I got my period before Marnie did, so I was showing her up again. I'll admit, I did brag a little and rub it in her face, because it was always fun to be better than Marnie in any way I could.

Even my first period came with complications, horrible cramps and excessive bleeding, as if my body were screaming at me to stop it somehow. *With what? Some magic spell? Getting bit by a vampire?* It didn't want to be a woman, and it didn't want to be real, because being real, and being independent and full of self, was a frightening thing you get punished for. For my part, I didn't want to be a woman, either. I wanted to stay a baby. When you're a baby, everything you do is adorable, no matter how stupid it is. Everyone loves you. I once lay down on Phyllis's lap to snuggle at a Halloween party, pushed up one of her enormous boobs and told everyone I was "fluffing my pillows." They nearly pissed themselves with laughter because I was little.

So from the start, my period was unwelcome. It made me more of an outcast, and it made me feel sick.

I remember hearing a lot about it in our sex education classes—which New York State was very serious about, to their credit—and the ladies who taught those classes seemed to think it was a wonderful thing. "It's a magical process," said one of them, because it was our body preparing itself to be a woman and a mother. I tried to imagine being a mother, with a little baby inside of me, and the thought seemed bizarre, like those Egyptian carvings of queens with fully formed humans in their stomachs. I wasn't sure it would ever be right for me.

Then there is the added genetic component. I don't know if my mother was ever aware of just how big a problem her period was, or that she had an unfortunate set of genes that made her Serotonin receptors intensely susceptible to the presence of the many hormones that course through the body after ovulation and before menstruation. Or maybe they were still calling this shit "hysteria" back then, I don't know. She passed these bum genes on to me, and though I knew nothing of this phenomenon—and wouldn't be able to put a name to it until my late twenties—I would soon begin to feel its frightening effect on my life, as I dipped in and out of madness about every twenty-eight days.

Of course, Marnie didn't get those genes, that likable bitch.

MY CYCLE, DAY 25—THE DAY OF MILD TALENT LOSS

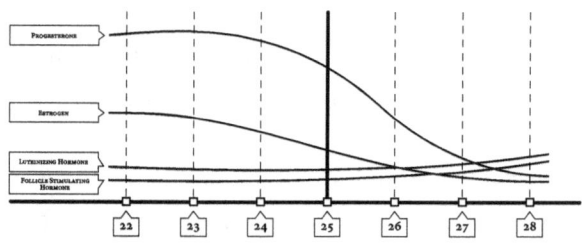

It's later afternoon on a Tuesday, in the dead of winter, and I am sitting in my PJs at the folding card table I use for a desk, working on a logo for an inflatable jump house company called Jump Zone.

The client seems to like the logo, but wants "more color." I'm having a hard time figuring out which green to use, because if

I go too lime, it clashes with the orange, but if I head toward the seafoam direction, the palette feels too nineties. These are the puzzles that torture designers, the things that literally no one but designers notice or give a fuck about.

But I am definitely feeling "off." For an hour or more, I've been pulling the "hue slider" back and forth between a hundred variations of green, unhappy with any green, really.

A terrible thought occurs to me: maybe I have no talent any more.

Murph is curled up on the sofa a few feet away. Every now and then, she comes over to my chair and makes little chirps and hops that express her current wants and needs—another trip to the dog park, a walk, or food. She pretty much always wants food, but she's had all of these things in spades today, and I have a deadline.

"No, no," I say, kissing her head in the divot between her eyes. "Mommy has to work."

She trots back to the sofa, rolls herself into a ball and emits a pissy sigh.

"I know, Murpher," I say. "I'm the worst."

I rub my face with my hands and think about what to do next.

WHY BOTHER, ERIN? YOUR TALENT IS GONE.

I pour a glass of wine and sit down next to Murph on the sofa. Her tail thumps into the cushion as I rub her soft belly and wonder if I could ever be happy as a graphic designer. I'm clearly no good at it, and I had never wanted to be a designer anyway.

"So why the fuck am I doing this, Murph?" I ask.

She doesn't answer, because she's a dog, so I finish my wine and go for another glass in the kitchen. Murph follows me there, hoping for a chewy, which she begs for and gets. I pour a bit too much wine into my glass and briefly consider that this night may not end well. This will be the last of my rational thoughts for a while.

By ten o'clock, I have a new career, and I have spent several hundred dollars I cannot afford to spend on an enormous colored pencil set and several pads of pricey paper. And wine, I bought wine too.

I reason I have not lost my ability to design; I am simply not well suited for the profession. My problem is that I never truly believed in myself and did what I wanted to do, which was to be an artist of some sort.

So I am no longer a designer. I am a children's book author, and I will write and illustrate the greatest story ever told, the story of the love between an otter mom and her little pup.

EXAMPLE: MOM'S CYCLE, DAY 26

I'm walking home from school with my viola on a warm fall

day, swinging it back and forth to quell the boredom. I'm angry that I am walking home alone, because I had to stay after school and practice viola with the rest of the orchestra, and I'm even angrier that I still have to play viola, which I have never liked, and can't for the life of me make a nice sound come out of. It's been five years since I started, and all I make is: *screech, ratch, screech.*

I decide I will walk down the middle of the street, because I'm pissed off. I kick acorns into the gutter as hard as I can, or sometimes I stomp on them with my Chucks.

It's about four thirty when I finally get home, and it's already starting to get dark. I chuck my viola into the den, and then go to the kitchen to make a snack. I don't notice Mom sitting in the dark in the living room. She's not reading the paper or a magazine, and she's not watching television like she usually does. She is simply sitting on a sofa in the dark looking at me.

"I saw you," she says to me, no hello or how was your day. "I saw you walking down the middle of the street like trash."

I lie, immediately. No I wasn't. Wait, how did she see me? Wait, what is going on here?

"You're lying," she says.

She looks at me, her face flat, and I look back until I can't anymore. It's an alpha move. I look at the wall next to her, the floor, the front door and then my feet, and at that point, I'm whipped.

"I'm always watching you," says Mom.

MY CYCLE, DAY 26—THE DAY PARANOIA SETS IN

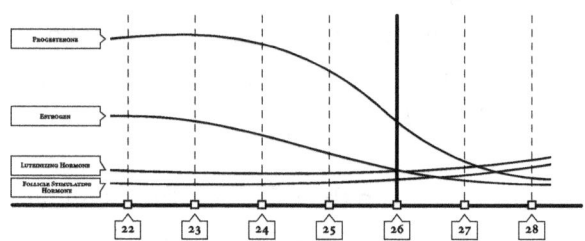

Murph wakes me up at seven thirty so I can be ready to drop her kibble in her bowl at eight o'clock. She chirps, stomps on my belly, and then licks every part of my face.

I have a terrible headache, and can't recall going to bed the night before.

I put my shoes on and take Murph out for a walk, and then I dump a cup of kibble into her bowl, which she waits impatiently in a sitting position for, with two long streams of drool hanging out of the sides of her mouth that flap around in the breeze of the ceiling fan. I tell her to shake, and she slaps her left socked paw into my hand, and when I say she can eat, she attacks the bowl, inhaling her kibble in under a minute, her rabies vaccination tag clanging against the metal rim.

I go to make a pot of coffee and notice that my kitchen countertops are stained with something. There's a top on the floor in the corner, the top I was wearing last night, and now it is covered in red splotches. I look up and see that my kitchen ceiling is covered in purplish streaks, and then I have a horrible memory from the prior night of not being terribly good at otter drawing, and deciding that another bottle of wine would help, which I tried to open with my crappy old corkscrew. I tore the cork in half and then—not knowing what to do, and desperate for more wine (and drunk)—I slammed a butter knife into the trapped bit of cork to push it into the bottle and release the wine, which is absolutely what happened. Except that the wine was released from the bottle in what could be called an explosion, and sprayed the ceiling, my body, and just about every surface in my kitchen.

It takes me hours to clean it up.

When I'm done, I am exhausted, and I make a pot of coffee so that I will have the energy to start drawing otters. I hover at the kitchen island, thinking about what I will draw.

Will my otters be river otters? The kind with the cute tails and naughty faces? Or will they be sea otters, those fluffy doe-eyed clam crackers you can't help but love? The ones that hold hands as they float around on their backs.

I had once seen a nature special about a single sea otter mom who put her pup on her belly and snuggled her to bond. I had lost my damn mind crying at that, but then, I had PMS at the time.

I'm pretty irrational when I have PMS. I wonder when it will come again?

The coffeepot peters out in one long gurgle. I pull my most treasured mug out of the dishwasher and pour myself a cup.

Then I go to the pantry to find my box of fake sweetener, and I'm pretty puzzled when I look inside and find nothing in it.

Huh.

I sit down to draw at my table, and though I sketch otter after otter, they don't seem to be coming out in any way that can be called "adorable."

THAT'S BECAUSE YOU HAVE NO TALENT, ERIN.

I slam my pencil down in frustration and think about cheese a little bit, and then I stare into a corner of my apartment for an indeterminate amount of time, simply because it feels pleasurable to do it.

My phone rings, and I feel frightened. I wonder if it's a bill collector, or if I am in trouble somehow.

Why would I be in trouble? What a weird thought.

I sit back in my chair and stretch my arms over my head. My spine cracks and pops a little, providing just a bit of relief, and I have an interesting thought:

Maybe I need a change of venue to become inspired?

I put my shoes on and pack up my tools and pad, and then I head to the Starbucks down the street where I know there will be hot coffee, plenty of sweetener, and that attractive barista, Javier—the one with the thick black hair and the full lips who's always nice to me when I go there, the one who smiled a little when our pinky fingers touched during a cash handover a month ago.

⌇

"It's *so* nice to see you again," I say to Javier with great emphasis on the "so" at the register as he hands me a venti and I drop a dollar into his Plexiglas tip cup. I say it a little desperately, and almost immediately I'm embarrassed.

NO ONE WANTS YOU, ERIN. YOU'RE CRAZY.

I sweeten my coffee and sit down to work at a little table in the back. Hours pass. I sketch a little, examine the sketching, find it to be not good at all, and then erase it and start over. My frustration builds into a funk of coffee-smelling sweat on all parts of my body, even my face. Every drawing of an otter is done atop the dents of the five terrible otter drawings that came before it. My otters, *I cannot get them right*. Two hours later, this is the equivalent of my day of work in total:

BECAUSE YOU HAVE NO TALENT, ERIN. EVERYONE KNOWS THIS.

Javier comes by my table to sweep up crumbs from the floor, and at one point, he leans his broom handle in the direction of my pad and says, "You're very good."

"Thanks," I say, wondering why his name tag says "Tim."

He looks down at my legs sort of quizzically, and I wonder if I haven't spilled coffee on myself or something. This isn't the case, which ought to relieve me, but in actuality doesn't, because in looking down at my legs I notice that I am wearing a gigantic pair of velour leopard-print pajama bottoms in a Starbucks, and most regrettably, I have paired these pants with a Hooters Las Vegas T-shirt. I have never been to Las Vegas, nor do I frequent Hooters restaurants, and so I have no idea where this shirt came from.

I rush home in my giant pants, my fingers spread out over the Hooters logo on my chest, my mind aflutter with paranoid thoughts. *Why is my life falling apart? Will I ever feel good again?*

I still don't know I have PMS.

EXAMPLE: MOM'S CYCLE, DAY 27

Some of my favorite memories of my family are the hot summer nights Dad would grill dinner on the Weber and we would all eat together at the picnic table in the backyard. Mom would make her famous macaroni salad and we would have sweet corn we bought fresh from the farm at a roadside stand in the country. Marnie and I would shuck the corn into a bucket, and when it came time to eat it, Mom would let us drown our ears in butter—a special treat. Mom's Day 27 example happened on one of these nights.

She isn't that out of sorts, but I do notice she seems a little off when she's especially short with me, snapping at things I don't quite recognize as being the usual in terms of what's snap worthy, like talking, or moving, or just generally being around her.

It should be noted that Mom has put on some pounds as of late, and though she is still a great beauty, she hates herself a bit more than usual.

When we sit down to eat at the picnic table we eat in tense silence. Mom mentions to dad that she has signed up for Weight Watchers and will be going to meetings soon, and Dad—the dumbass—says something very stupid about her not needing Weight Watchers classes, because weight loss is easy. You just eat less and go jogging. She doesn't go jogging anymore, and that's probably the problem. Oh Dad, you *dumbass.*

At this, Mom becomes a wild animal.

Her eyes widen and become frightening, as she slams both her fists down on one slat of the picnic table and our plates reverberate in response.

"I'M TRYING!" she screams at full volume, before picking up an ear of corn and launching it at one of two possible targets—my father or me—because the corn splits the distance between our heads at just shy of Randy Johnson fastball speed and lands twenty feet away in the neighbors' yard.

Mom runs into the house, sobbing into her hands.

MY CYCLE, DAY 27—THE DAY OF DAIRY

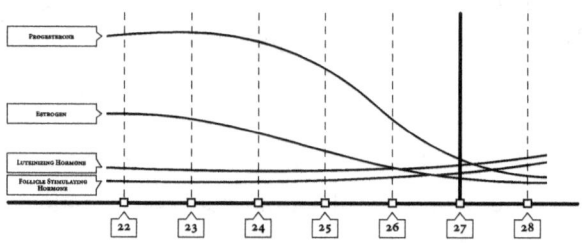

"Just give me a couple minutes," I moan to Murph, who's bouncing up and down on my chest. She wedges her snout under my neck and pushes me upright, a maneuver I'm calling "The Snout Doze." There is no sleeping past eight o'clock now that Murph is in my life. No, there is too much fun to be had, and too many exciting new treats to eat.

During our morning walk I notice that my hands look odd. I hold one up for inspection while Murph does her business. It is nearly twice the normal size, and though I try my best to make a fist with it, I can't. Not fully, at least. I am gobsmacked as I make indentations in my hand flesh that stay there and then slowly fade away, as if my hands were made of memory foam.

I brew coffee, find the empty box of sweetener and burst into tears.

ANOTHER EXAMPLE: MOM'S CYCLE, DAY 27

I'm never more frightened of Mom than when she is mad at Marnie. Me? Not a big deal, but when she's mad at my sister, the shit has hit the fan.

It is spring, and we are driving to some location I cannot remember where. Marnie came home earlier in the day with a midterm report card for Mom to inspect and sign, because she currently has a D average in English class. This is strange because Marnie is a good student—especially in English—and has never gotten less than a B in it.

I watch from the back seat of the family station wagon as Mom screams at Marnie, the car swerving wildly back and forth, nicking trashcans and bouncing off curbs. Marnie is sobbing into her hands, stopping every so often to dry off her face with a sleeve and to explain to Mom she has some missing assignments, and when she completes them and hands them in, she won't have a D in English.

"I'M GONNA HOLD YOU BACK A YEAR!" screams mom.

She swerves to miss a parked car. Marnie sobs.

At Starbucks, Javier seems frightened. I wonder if he has noticed my memory-foam hands.

I sit down and draw the equivalent of this psychotic monstrosity, a creature born out of frustration and many, many erasures:

Javier smiles from behind the pastry case, his beautiful mocha face so soothing to look at. I lean back, put my pencil down, and consider what it would be like to date him. *How does one date such a normal man, a man who is kind and reciprocates your affections—a man who doesn't throw furniture at you for not putting the nail clippers back in the nail clipper spot at the specified nail clipper angle?*

BUT YOU DON'T DESERVE THAT KIND OF MAN, ERIN.

I watch him stock pastries and fantasize about a future with him. *What would our life be like?*

We'd get married on a tropical beach, just the two of us—so long as there are pictures for mom—and we'll have a daughter together we named Angel, pronounced "An-hel" in the way of his people, and when she's two or three, and the time is right, we'll have a son named Seamus, pronounced "Shay-mus" in the way of my people. I'd help Angel with her art projects and Javier—or Tim or whatever—would help Seamus with his math and we would be so happy as a couple. The kids would be happy too.

Would the kids really be happy? Do they have any idea how much I do for them?

I look down and notice that I am wearing the same gigantic pair of velour leopard-print pants and Hooters Las Vegas T-shirt.

I wonder when I showered last, and then I can only think about one thing: *ice cream.*

PMS eating is a strange thing. I often find myself not thinking of food at all in the beginning stages—the day of talent loss and the day of paranoia. It's not uncommon for me to eat nothing for days, save for coffee and a little snack, which my body will compensate for in disgusting fashion.

I once saw a video on the internet of the ocean receding off the coast of Thailand, being pulled out to some sucking force miles out to sea, before being violently hurled in tsunami form back at the beachfront of the town nearby and just about anything else it wanted to destroy.

That's what PMS eating is like.

I am wrapped in a blanket on the sofa next to Murph, whose drool streams are in full force, as she looks at me, looks down at my pint of Ben and Jerry's Oatmeal Cookie, looks at me, looks down at my pint—and so on and so forth. I carve a spoonful out of the pint and into my mouth, and then I let Murph lick the flavors off the spoon. It's probably not the most hygienic thing to do with a dog who, only recently, overcame a horrendous roundworm infection, but I can't say no to those sparkly meatball eyes.

In between spoonfuls I scratch the soft fur behind her ears and tell her how much I love her.

I had considered showering and changing out of my horrid leopard pants and Hooters tee before making the trek to Subway, but to be honest, I was still very hungry after eating the pint of ice cream, and grooming myself seemed like a complex thing to do, with a lot of steps I didn't even want to think about.

I regret this decision, now, as I walk through my fashionable Chicago neighborhood at six o'clock, just in time to be taken in by the horde of young preppies on their way home from sensible jobs in sleek boots and snappy wool coats cinched at the middle. The wind billows my leopard pants, which flap about my legs, clownishly, and people point at them, snort and laugh at me like the kids did back in high school—the cool kids who mocked me for tap dancing and flag twirling.

I feel much better when I reach the Subway, at which I order a six-inch sandwich with extra cheese. I eat this sandwich on my sofa with Murph, and with every bite I admit I feel much better. Nutrients begin to work their way back into my depleted system, and when I am done eating my sandwich, I put my shoes on and go back to Subway for another.

It is while eating this second sandwich that I take stock of the many days' events—the job quitting and the pants and the obsession with dairy—and I finally realize I am suffering from PMS.

"Oh," I say. "Duh."

I lean to my side on the sofa and take a light nine-hour nap.

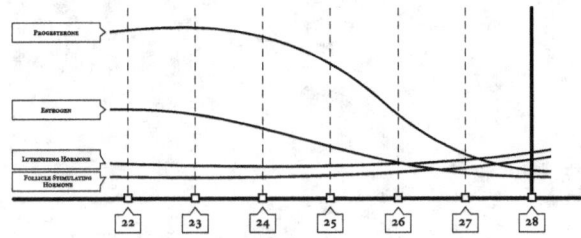

The cramps wake me up around six o'clock in the morning. I am still on the sofa, still wearing the pants and tee, with what feels like several bricks in my stomach—the 1.5 feet of Subway sandwiches I ate the night before.

I take a shower and put on fresh clothes.

I go back to being a graphic designer.

I LIVE IN ARIZONA NOW...

...by way of both New York and Los Angeles, because I still believe
if I can run fast enough, I can outrun all my problems.

This is not the case, of course. (And this is never ever possible, by the way. Save your money.)

I still have all my bad habits, but I continue to write, and it keeps my head above water.

I begin to see doctors for my problems, not to *talk about* them, but to get the right medication to make me less aware of them—the right pill, or patch, or injection, or shock therapy if need be—that I can use to rid me of my wrong feelings and finally be functional.

The Tower

A recurring dream from childhood

I'm standing in a field full of waist-high grass. The sky is swirling with angry clouds and the moon is full. Dad is next to me, and I reach up for his hand, but it's a hologram and I can't hold it.

Off in the distance is a tower, black and decrepit. I can see pits of decay in it as it climbs into the sky in ragged spikes.

Dad walks toward the tower and I follow along, but the grass is thick with oily slime and my shoes get stuck in it.

I can hear witchy laughter from the top of the tower, and then a shrill voice saying "Erin…"

"I don't want to go up!" I say to Dad. "Let's go. Let's go away from here."

I grab his arm and my hands slip through it.

I start to climb up the tower and the cackling gets louder. I hear my name again and again: "Erin…" My heart thumps.

When I reach the top, there is nothing there. I look out over the edge and see Dad, far below. I hear footsteps behind me and then laughter.

FRAUDEM
THE ALIEN/HUMAN HYBRID MAN
FROM 300 YEARS INTO THE FUTURE

I'm sitting on the couch of my RV drinking a cup of coffee and doing a crossword puzzle from the day's newspaper. There's a blue heron family living in the oak tree above me, and the babies are squawking for breakfast. Cold water from the Colorado Plateau bubbles over the rocks in the creek nearby. Sometimes there's a mountain lion print or two in the creek bed sand in the morning.

Murph wakes me at seven, now, and we walk to the convenience store up the hill, take in the beauty of this new place we live, and get a paper, a to-go cup of coffee, and one cheese stick I give to Murph. She seems to like Colby Jack most, but let's face it—she'll eat anything. She's four years old now—a very good girl—and spry as a mountain goat. Our new home is banked by red canyons on all sides, and when Murph and I go on our hikes together, she scampers up seemingly unclimbable canyon walls with ease on her hunt for lizards, her ordinarily white socks pink with dust.

I got the RV back in Los Angeles with the intention of travelling from town to town, and never really settling anywhere, which in hindsight I'll admit was another of my attempts to "move escape" my problems by moving my location—this time continually, like I'm a fugitive on the run. I got as far as this batty little new age town in Arizona, and decided that I both hated driving an RV and enjoyed being here.

I am not sure what to think of the people here. When I first get to know them, they are quite kind and congenial. Everyone here seems focused on healing, and the process of bettering oneself in various new age hippie ways, and they're more than willing to share what they've learned with you—how we are all a part of one consciousness experiencing itself subjectively, and therefore love is all that matters—but tell them you eat meat, and they tell you to eat shit and die. Well they tell you the new age equivalent of that, which is "you have toxic energy."

There's also an unfortunate *alien component* to the culture here.

To be fair, Southwest alien/human breeding culture was not born in this little town; it was simply perfected here. I learn about it in bits and pieces from the townsfolk I meet, who are surprisingly casual about the whole thing, as if this were happening in every town in America. Quite simply, aliens are abducting humans—usually older, post-menopausal humans about my parents' age—to extract their sperm and eggs, which they use in some advanced breeding process to make alien/human hybrid babies that float around on ships in the sky. It's considered something of an honor to be selected for this process, I'm told. You have to have something called an "advanced consciousness." Many residents have alien babies.

Even the mayor has a circular ring of rocks in his backyard meant to mark a potential landing space his alien/human babies can park their ship should they ever decide to visit him, and it's not at all uncommon to see residents wear crystal necklaces they use to communicate with their alien babies. If the necklace spins clockwise, the answer is "yes," and if it spins counterclockwise, the answer is "no."

There's a knock at my RV door, as much as such doors can be knocked on. There's a hollow crack at my RV door, I should say. I open it and see my neighbor, a lovely lady named SueEllen, with long, calico-colored hair and an always-cheerful disposition. She's a polarity therapist from New Hampshire, and she has a sweet little dog named Scruffy that Murph loves to play with.

SueEllen holds up a crudely done flyer with new age graphics on it. The liberal use of the "Papyrus" font in these parts is something that will haunt me for years.

"Do you want to go see a man channel an alien/human hybrid named Fraudem who lives three hundred years into the future?" she asks.

"Yes," I say. "Yes, I very much do."

✦ ✦ ✦

These sorts of things happen in circus tents, apparently. Nice circus tents, like the kind you rent for outdoor weddings, the white ones with the little plastic windows and overhead twinkle lights. The land out here is known for its sweat lodges. Gurus hold wealth creation seminars and such.

The crowd is full of older people in loose linen from Chico's, with chunky necklaces and loaded Pandora bracelets jingling in excitement. There are coolers full of special water in three locations, water which has been blessed with the energy of love, light, or Christ consciousness by a local shaman. I am drinking a cup of love and watching the portly older gentleman who will channel Fraudem, the alien/human hybrid man, as he eagerly chats up an attractive brunette half his age with "desperate for answers" doe eyes.

The ladies seated in front of me are wondering if Fraudem will finally reveal himself. They've been to five of these events, and though he promised he may make an appearance, he never really did. One lady pulls the crystal from her neck and asks it if Fraudem will show. She spins the crystal clockwise, and the two do a little celebration dance in their chairs.

There are several people in this tent having full conversations with necklaces.

The channel man says goodbye to his brunette, and takes the

stage. He introduces himself, and tells us that he is nothing more than a telephone for an alien; it is Fraudem who does all the work, and it should be Fraudem who is celebrated.

There's a collective coo as he announces that Fraudem has flown his spaceship directly over our skies in preparation for the day so that their connection is totally secure. I wonder if this sort of thing is like Wi-Fi, and whether we will have to shut this man down and restart him again?

Then he begins the channeling process, which cracks me up. He removes his glasses, drops his chin to his chest and is silent for almost a minute, before launching into a series of strange, jerky movements and weird sounds like "Ah" and "Brrrp." There is no offensive screeching, like any child of the nineties who dialed up AOL would recognize, but the similarity between this man and a modem is noticeable.

Finally, he sits up straight as can be and chirps, Kermit the Frog–like:

"Hello everyone, and thank you for your love!"

The tent erupts as Fraudem groupies welcome their hero.

When I had first walked into this tent and taken in the table full of merch—the many Fraudem-themed CDs, posters, T-shirts, and swag items on which one could blow all their hard-earned Reiki, or massage therapy, or tarot reading money—I had felt sad and also a little angry, but as it turns out, Fraudem is a really nice dude.

He talks about time being an illusion humans cling too tightly to, and how we are too fearful to access our boundless ability to love. He tells us that cancer is the disease of "I can't, sir," and that love of self and others is all that is necessary to cure it. Should I ever get cancer I will be sure to combine this treatment plan with aggressive chemotherapy. He tells us that we should follow our excitement to whatever passions or play or joy we can imagine for ourselves, and at this point I have decided that I quite like this alien dude who lives three hundred years into the future.

Sadly, Fraudem does not come to visit us.

When the channeling ends, SueEllen and I head up the hill with the linen ladies to walk the labyrinth, which I suspect is nothing more than an alien/human hybrid baby landing pad.

I look around at these weird people who are so comfortable with their weirdness and think I could probably learn a thing or two. *Let's stay here*, I say to myself. *Could we? Could we be weird on purpose?*

Let's get weird.

I used to see a doctor in Tampa for my badness. He never wanted to discuss my life problems, and that was just fine by me. I'd visit him in a short skirt and all the makeup I owned, and he'd ask, "What drugs you want?" while looking up that skirt and then give me free sample packs of anything he had on hand. I'd take them all, feel like a zombie, and not shit for a week.

"All life haf' stress," he'd say. "What drugs you want?"

In Chicago, I finally sought out legitimate talk therapy, or so I thought. I bought a session with the only psychologist I could afford who practiced at a city-subsidized facility in a half-abandoned building near Cabrini-Green. He was gray haired, and wore a puffy, outdoorsy vest, and as is common with men of his age, it was impossible for him to think about anything but his own immediate needs, which happened to be, at the time the setting up of his brand-new, city-subsidized Macintosh.

I installed his system software for him while telling him about my badness, and when I was done, he very unempathically said, "It sounds like you're bipolar, so there's really nothing anyone can do for you. You'll just have to be on meds your whole life."

It turned out that if you didn't have bipolar disorder, but wanted to get bipolar medication, it was a breeze, but like the many forms of birth control I'd been prescribed over the years to treat my period problems, the bipolar meds did shit all to help me, and so months later—after a forty-pound weight gain and no appreciable difference in mood—I took myself off the meds, and proceeded to both vomit and shake for a week.

I go to Dr. Granger on a Tuesday. I don't know why, but this is something I remember perfectly. It is a Tuesday at two o'clock, and I ride my bicycle there in the July heat, so when I arrive to Dr. Granger's fancy and expensive office, I have massive sweat rings in the pits of my tee. Dr. Granger wears a Diane von Fürstenberg wrap dress and patent leather kitten heels. There's a Japanese print of a samurai above her head in a bamboo frame and it's worth more than the totality of my being.

I feel profoundly out of place in my dirty gray tee and shorts.

I found Dr. Granger on the internet one frightening afternoon during which I telephone-fought with a piece of shit ex-boyfriend and upon hanging up, heard **THIS VOICE** tell me I am "completely unworthy of being loved." As tired as I am of that voice's bullshit, I decided to punch myself in the head a whole lot and scream "GET OUT," again and again, which would have been more acceptable if I hadn't currently been driving about seventy miles per hour on a freeway and swerving recklessly from lane to lane with my left hand, my eyes so full of tears I could barely see the lane markers. I exited the freeway and went to a gas station bathroom to clean up, and when I looked myself dead in the eyes in the bathroom mirror, I said "I am fucking done with you."

My thinking is, Dr. Granger, being the most learned and most expensive professional in this batty new age town, can properly diagnose me and prescribe me the pill I need to take away all my wrong feelings.

Trouble is, Dr. Granger doesn't understand what this story is about.

I tell her I am bad and burdensome. I say I am crazy and that my poor, long-suffering family deserves much better. I tell her I date monsters and throw up on purpose, and that I drink to knock myself out. I wake up outside, and in strange places. I wake up wondering how I got home. Sometimes it's a miracle I wake up at all.

And Dr. Granger always says, "Tell me about your parents."

So I do. I tell her that my mother is a blonde beauty who was a perfect mother. She was the president of the PTA and she did everything for my sister and me. I tell her my father is an amazing man, who reads a book a week and hunts and fishes and scuba dives and skis.

And Dr. Granger always says, "No, but really tell me about your parents."

There's something about Dr. Granger that feels oddly comfortable to me, as if I've known her in a past life. She's an older lady with a soft, round face, an Anna Wintour type-bob of black hair, and a lot of makeup. Too much makeup. She wears a shit ton of makeup, like much younger girls from Scottsdale with blackened raccoon eyes and neon-red lips. She is painfully thin and often appears to be falling asleep in session. I wonder if it's because she's hungry and then I chalk it up to me being tiresome.

One thing is certain: she will *not* prescribe me pills.

"There is nothing wrong with you," she says.

How can I make her understand?

One whole year.

That's how long this expensive dance between
Dr. Granger and me goes on, with me trying to get
my crazy pills to be empty and her saying I'm not
crazy, I simply need to talk about my anger toward
my parents, who are perfect. We cumulatively
spend hours in tense silence, as Murph sits outside
the picture window of her fancy office, scowling at
Granger through the glass with a genuine and
pure dislike I find puzzling.

*Dr. Granger only wants to help me. Usually Murph
is an excellent judge of character.*

the bad ones

Sometimes the power of story humbles me. Even in this moment I am about to mention—when I am stubborn and stiff and wholly unwilling to consider any other explanation for why I have problems—I hear Granger tell this story and it creates a storm of thought in me that changes me forever.

One day in session, Granger asks me if I've ever heard of the African witch children, and of course I haven't, and tell her as much.

She tells me that there are certain tribes in Africa who have a superstitious custom of banishing witch children. When bad things happen within the tribe, and there is great stress—death, disease, famine—they have to be explainable. So they identify a child who is a little different because of a disability, or a unique gift, or because they just don't fit in with the rest of the children, and they label that child a witch and banish him or her from the tribe. If the child doesn't die from exposure or starvation, it is murdered, and then the tribe is clean again.

It's like that goat from the bible, the one the tribe lays their sins upon and banishes to the desert to die.

It's Halloween night, 1982, and I'm sitting dejectedly on the back of Simon, my rocking horse, wondering how much longer I'll have to wait for the candy. I'm brooding, per usual, because I don't like my costume, and because Marnie's costume is so much better. Of course I'm also brooding because riding Simon had been a world of fun until recently, when Bobby Banona—the surly teenager with the special needs problems from across the street—shit his pants on Simon's back.

Sometimes I wonder if riding Simon will ever be the same again.

Marnie is sitting in the tall chair in the kitchen looking adorable in her ballet tights and a white T-shirt. My mother is carefully applying blue eye shadow to her lids with an applicator sponge, and dang it, she looks pretty. Of course, I would never tell her that.

I want eyeshadow too. I want peachy pink slashes on my cheeks like the ladies from the videos on MTV. I want to be a pretty lady like Mom with long blonde hair, the kind of lady everybody looks at when she drinks her Diet Tab out of striped straws on the beach in a sleek swimsuit or bikini, and points her shapely legs and feet just so in the most pretty positions before she goes to outer space or the moon because she's an astronaut.

Mom loves to brush Marnie's hair in the morning, and style it into all sorts of clever, golden twists, and braids and pigtails with the wooden-handled brush of doom she uses to smack my behind for sassing her. I hate that thing. Mom's face is so at ease and satisfied as she wraps the golden strands around her fingers, thinking about what she wants to create. They even collaborate sometimes in disgusting baby voices.

"What would you wike to have today, princess? Do you want pigtails?"

"Yes, Mommy," says Marnie, who always says yes to Mom.

When Mom is finished she takes out her special tin of ribboned barrettes and lets Marnie pick out the one she thinks will look best with her outfit (and corrects Marnie when she's wrong). I am not allowed to wear any of the barrettes, because of an incident earlier in the year when Mom swept my short brown hair to one side—short because it's difficult and tangles—and then secured it with a compensatory barrette that had a playful elephant button and purple ribbons, and I got pissed off and threw that shit in the gutter out front.

Mom tosses the shadow back in her maroon, flower-print makeup bag and roots for something else. I'm not allowed to touch the makeup bag either, because I once snuck into Mom's room while she was ironing and painted myself up like the sexy ladies who kiss Dr. Webber on General Hospital, and when I was finished, I knocked her sunset peach blusher onto the floor and cracked it into shards. I tried to blame it on my cat, Soupy, but Mom knew it was me, of course.

Mom paints Marnie's lips a coral shade and has her blot them on a tissue. She caps the lipstick and tosses it in the bag, and then she pulls a tissue from the box on the counter and folds it in half. She places the tissue between Marnie's lips and says "blot." Marnie presses her lips down onto the tissue.

She puts her makeup away and hands Marnie a little mirror. I see her face light up with joy as she admires her own reflection.

I sigh. She does look very pretty.

There's a curling iron plugged in nearby on the counter, and Mom taps the barrel of it to test if it's hot enough to use. She pulls my sister's hair to one side, isolates a section of it, and then carefully wraps it around the barrel. The strand begins to steam and sizzle, and then it unravels into a beautiful blonde spiral. Mom sets the iron on the counter and sprays the curl with a can of Aqua Net.

She taps it a little, and it bounces in response.

Mom follows suit with each strand of Marnie's hair until her head is covered in glorious ringlets. She runs her fingers through them to break them up and then they coo about how pretty she looks. Mom hoists her from the chair by her pits and tells her to go put her robe on.

Mom calls me into the kitchen, and puts me in the chair. She tells me how cute I am as she taps the tip of my nose. She tucks my hair behind my ears as much as it will go and pulls up the hood of my red sweatshirt, straightening the two little horns she's sewed to the top. She backs up a few feet and takes me in. Her brow furrows and she begins to root through her maroon makeup bag.

Blue eye shadow? I wonder, excitedly.

She pulls out an eyeliner, reddish brown in color, and draws with it on my upper lip, standing back and looking over her work before coming back in to draw with it over my brows and then under my chin in a cold, waxy "V." She busts out laughing as she hands me the mirror. I look like Snidely Whiplash, for God's sake.

I try to think of the candy. There will be candy soon. I try to imagine which candy I will eat first. *I love a good Crunch bar, but if I get a Snickers, all bets are off.*

Dad comes up from the basement with a sparkly halo and wing contraption he's made out of wire and tinsel, and Marnie holds up her arms so that he can slip it onto her like a backpack. He adjusts the halo part a little and then he and Mom stand back and admire their work.

Mom stands us against the living room wall for pictures. "Smile," she says.

I think of Skittles and then I smile.

One of the things I love most about Murph is that she keeps it simple. She loves love and she loves food, and that's what she's about. You can't always count on life being predictable, but you can always count on Murph loving love and loving food.

For better or for worse, *Murph is Murph*.

We're driving home together from a trip to the fancy dog park in the neighboring city about forty-five minutes away. We can't always make time for such trips, but it had been a rare temperate morning, and so I thought I'd spoil Murph. She spent hours with new dog friends zooming in joyous circles, diving into the pond, and chasing tennis balls until she was blue in the face and simply had no more fuel left in her tank.

The light ahead turns red, and I come to a stop. Murph sticks her head out of the back window, and I watch in the rearview mirror as her snout tips up and her nostrils flare. There is a steak house up the road on the right-hand side, and the air is full of delicious roasting meat.

When the light turns green, I turn onto the freeway on-ramp and hear a commotion in the back of the car.

I look behind me. Murph isn't there. A feeling of panic rips through me.

Murph jumped out the window onto a freeway on-ramp.

OH, GODDAMN IT, MURPH!

I hit the gas and fly to the next exit, and in a series of horn slams, red-light runs, and illegal turns over sidewalks—all while screaming at people to get the fuck out of my way—I make my way back to Murph. My mind is full of horrible images of her flattened in the middle of the freeway, but the road is clear and there's no sign of her. I park my car sideways in the middle of the on-ramp and begin to search the brush. The traffic piles up behind my car and people begin to lay on their horns.

"MURPHY!" I scream into the brush by the on-ramp. "MURPHY!"

She doesn't come.

A man opens his car door and stands up. "Get out of the way!" he yells.

"MURPHY!" I scream. She doesn't come.

I call out again and again, but she doesn't come, and then I begin to realize she's not going to come so long as I scream. She's hiding because she knows that when Mom yells, she is in trouble.

I lower my voice and call out to her in a singsong way I use just before I give her delicious treats. "Mur-phy," I chirp, trying to sound as cheery as I can, though my heart is beating out of my chest. Drivers make long, angry honks, and people scream. "Mur-phy," I chirp.

I hear a rustling in the bushes, and then Murph sheepishly appears, shell-shocked from her fall, her eyes in a squint and her ears pinned back. There are sticks and clumps of dirt in her fur and burrs stuck to her tail. She's bleeding on her elbows from the road rash.

"Oh, Murph!" I say, bursting into tears. I scoop her up in my arms and carry her like a baby to the car, and when the angry drivers see this, they stop the honking and the screaming, and they seem to understand the reason I parked sideways and blocked the on-ramp.

I take Murph home and wash the burrs from her fur. I wrap her elbows with gauze, and we snuggle all night long. I hold her in my arms, scratch the soft fur behind her ears, and I tell her how much I love her, and how I couldn't imagine life without her goofy face.

And then I never drive past a steak house with the windows down again.

It's been a trying day at the New York State Fair.

Earlier in the day, I tripped on an electrical cable and skinned my knee, which had to be bandaged by the nice cow doctor man. After that, Dad smacked my behind for sticking my tongue out at him when I wanted to pet the goats and everyone else had to pee, and it had been a record-breaking whooping, for sure. It easily bested the time Dad was reshingling the roof, and tossing the nails and old shingles and such onto my various play areas in the yard, and—totally put out by it—I had said, "Will somebody clean up around here?"

Also I didn't get to eat cheese curds because I had been naughty about the goats. Also this year's butter sculpture sucked.

So I am cranky, for sure, but then I see his fuzzy, precocious face propped on a pole in the market in a sea of a hundred other less fascinating monkey puppets because they are not my monkey soul mates. He's white and fluffy and we are meant to be together forever. I decide I must have him now, so I claw at my mother's leg and beg for the birthday money I've brought to the fair.

Mom pays the man at the stand, and he puts my monkey into a plastic bag, but as my monkey does not belong shrouded from the world in plastic, I rip him right back out again and slide him onto my hand. It's hot as Hades today at the fair, but I wear my new monkey puppet everywhere, my hand sweat building into a formidable funk inside of his synthetic fur, my anger melting into joy as we discover things together.

Already, I am in love. I will name him Fluffaduffle and we will have the best adventures together.

Fluff came along at a time in my life when I was feeling very angry, and acting on it regularly. My feelings weren't deemed "incorrect" yet, but they were certainly unwelcome. No, it was not okay to beat the shit out of Marnie when she told me I'd die of cancer if I touched my pee parts, and no, it was not alright to openly sass Mom. It was not okay for me to buy ten penny candies at the corner store down the street with three stolen packs of Starburst tucked into my drawers because the old man once said he liked to look at my Mom's "jugs" when she jogged. It was not alright when I kicked Danny Eagle in the nuts for throwing an ice ball at Marnie's head, and it was certainly not appropriate—when the boys in band made fun of Marnie's screechy violin playing—for me to tell them to shove their horns up their assholes.

(That's a word I learned from my Uncle JK just recently—who is my favorite uncle and says all sorts of fun swears around me—and though I technically don't know what an asshole is or looks like, I can tell from his tone when he talks about it that it's not the kind of hole I want to step in.)

When I learned anger was not okay, things became a bit scarier. The only thing worse than aggression is passive aggression. Sometimes at night, when we'd have our bath time, I'd wait for Marnie to shampoo her hair—which she always did with eyes closed—and then piss in the bath water. I'd giggle as I watched her scoop cup after cup of my pee onto her stupid blonde head.

Eventually, I realized I was pissing on myself, too, so I stopped.

But I find anger to be a very puzzling thing, because it feels good to get it out, but people tell you that you shouldn't do that. It feels terrible to keep it in, and the longer I do, the bigger the anger gets.

I don't know when it first occurred to me that Fluffaduffle was antisocial; I only know that while Fluff and I were very good friends—the best of friends, you could say—he really didn't care for the rest of my family at all.

Fluff and I are sitting at the tiny green table in the corner. He always holds the paper down to the table for me so I can color on it with my right hand. We're both snickering because Marnie is about to drink milk that has dirt in it.

Sometimes Fluff leaves tacks from the office on the living room sofa, and sometimes Marnie or Mom sits down on them and says "ouch," and then wonders how a tack got onto the sofa. I know it was Fluff, but I'd never rat on a friend.

Other times, Fluff does nasty stuff with their toothbrushes and puts them back in the toothbrush rack, and then the two of us laugh it up while they brush before bed.

Marnie has poured herself that glass for her afternoon snack of graham crackers, which she always cracks at the perforations and dips into the milk to soften before eating. Fluff knows that, and he also knows that he only has a few seconds to make the drop, which we've prepared for by pre-scooping some dirt ahead of time in the side yard. Now we wait patiently in the living room behind Simon the Shit Horse.

Then it is time. Marnie goes to the pantry for the crackers and we dash to the milk and drop about a sixteenth of a Dixie cup's worth of dirt into her milk, which we stir crudely with one of my fingers before running into the living room and sitting down to the green table again.

I wonder if we have done enough stirring. I wonder if the dirt has sunk to the bottom, or if it's sitting at the top in a big blob of evidence, but Fluff says that we did our best. We did all we could do and we should be proud of ourselves.

Marnie pads through the living room like a cat with her snack, hissing at us as she passes. She joins Mom in the den, who is folding the laundry and watching *General Hospital*. Fluff and I get up and hover in the doorway to the den, trying not to make any distracting movements or sounds. I hold in a breath and wait. Marnie pops her first graham cracker into two squares and then sets one down. She pops that square into two little rectangles and sets one down. Now she goes for the milk.

Here it is! Here is our reward.

She dips the little rectangle of sweet cracker into the milk and wiggles it slowly back and forth, to better absorb the cracker-softening milk, and yes, a sixteenth of a Dixie cup's worth of side yard dirt.

I can't hold in my laughter anymore. Fluff and I dart through the living room, the kitchen, the mudroom, and pound down the steps to the yard, where we erupt in belly laughter that takes ages to subside.

Then we go bat some honeybees into the siding.

🝆 🝆 🝆

It's a Saturday morning, and Fluff and I are waiting for him in the dark in the living room, like he waits for deer in the forest.

No sudden movements. No loud noises.

We're wrapped in two old afghans knitted by mean old Aunt Caroline, Grandma Phyllis's sister who calls people names and throws shit at them, and also wonders why we never go to see her in the old folks' home.

My toes are cold, but I'm heating my slippers on the heating vent in the corner, and when I put them back on, it will feel magical.

The television is on, and the volume is low. *Bozo's Circus* is on. I don't like Bozo, but I don't want to miss the start of Saturday morning cartoons.

Just then, I hear the floorboards creak above me and Fluff, and I am excited. I imagine him putting on his robe, slowly, methodically in the "big man" way he does it, and pushing his feet into his "big man" slippers, and heading down the stairs with thuds, solid, thick "big man" thuds, making the old wood whine under his weight.

I have been very clever. I have woken early and been quiet

and still, and now I get my special treat, which is to have him all to myself, no Marnie and no Mom.

Then he appears in the doorway to the living room and says, "Morning, Murph," his Irish eyes in half moons as he smiles at me. That's right, he smiles at me only. Just me. He comes over to me, leans down and kisses my head, and it is glorious.

"You want pancakes?" he asks.

"Yes," I say.

He heads into the kitchen, and I hear cupboards open. There are little clanging noises, and then I hear the sound of the pantry door squeak open. The rubber seal on the fridge door breaks, and then there are cracking noises of eggshells against a glass bowl. A fork thwaps against the glass and the coffee maker starts to gurgle. I can smell it now.

I get up and run toward the kitchen, hitting the linoleum at top speed and sliding expertly through the room in a quarter squat with Fluff at attention on my right hand. Dad laughs, as I suspected he would. I make Fluff chirp a little and Dad calls him an asshole.

Dad drops a lump of margarine onto the electric griddle and says, "You'll miss your cartoons."

I take off again in a series of slips as I try to get traction in my footies.

Fluff and I sit down in the living room again and watch *The Smurfs,* which is my favorite Saturday cartoon, save for *Scooby-Doo*. I like it when Scooby goes crazy for food snacks, and I like Velma because she's smart and sensible and solves all the crimes while everyone is gawking at Daphne's boobs.

The house fills with the scent of browning buckwheat pancakes, and the smell of it makes my mouth water. I wonder what Dad will put in them, and hope it will be chocolate chips. Marnie likes blueberries in her pancakes, and I think that's disgusting.

I hear another creaking sound, this time a much lighter one, and there is sinking in my chest.

Could it be over already?

Marnie appears at the bottom of the stairwell rubbing the sleep from her eyes. Her hair is a blonde mop of tangled curls as she strolls over to the living room, smirks at me, and struts into the kitchen to ruin my morning.

I hear my father say good morning to her and I compare it to the way he said good morning to me and find it slightly less enthusiastic. Perhaps it's just my imagination. I wonder if she got a kiss on the head, too, and if so, was it longer than mine?

I get up and tiptoe to the doorway of the kitchen, peeking inside to see what's going on. Marnie is sitting on the counter next to Dad, sipping from a cup—juice, probably. Why didn't I get juice? I like juice.

He seems happier now. *Is he happier?*

Dad spies me in the doorway. "Whatcha doin', Murph?"

"Nothin'," I say.

"Go watch your cartoons, and I'll bring you pancakes in a minute."

I set a wooden tray table in front of the television and try to watch an episode of *Scooby-Doo*. Dad comes around the corner with a plate of blueberry pancakes. He sets a fork and napkin down on my tray table, and hands me some juice in a tumbler. "Don't spill," warns Dad.

There's no syrup on my pancakes, so I take them back to the kitchen where I find Dad helping Marnie cut her pancakes into perfect little squares. I grab the syrup off the table and pour it onto my plate, and then I slam it back down onto the table, causing Marnie's fork to jiggle, and she says "Hey!"

Shut up.

I take my pancakes back to the living room and shove them into my face while I watch *Scooby-Doo*, sulk a little, and think about how gross blueberries are. I let my cat lick the rest of the syrup off the plate.

I watch Saturday morning cartoons until *The Snorks* comes on, because I can't stand *The Snorks*, and then Fluff and I think of things to do.

APPALACHIAN SKIING

FAMILY FUN TIME

Is it cycle day 27? I don't know. Sometimes it seems like Mom doesn't need a menstrual reason to be moody, because her moodiness problems are now much bigger than her period.

She's a vision in her crisp white ski suit, cinched at the waist with a belt. She wears a puffy hat and pair of white mittens, and her hair hangs in still-artful swoops, though the snow peppers it with bits of white.

We stand at the top of the ski slope putting our goggles on and situating our mittens into the handles of our poles. Then Dad takes off down the hill, skating to pick up speed, and I drop in behind him and lose Mom and Marnie.

Dad is up ahead of me, swooshing back and forth deftly, and I'm right behind him in a tuck, trying to catch up. He swerves over to the good snow on the right side of the slope between the tree line and the lift tower, where only the good skiers can go, and when he meets the top of the lip, he digs his right pole into hard pack, swings his skis left, and drops out of sight. I follow right along, dig my pole into the snow, and drop down with him.

We race to the bottom, and it is neck and neck, but I can never quite beat him there. I come to an exaggerated stop next to Dad, spraying him with snow as much as I can.

"Oh Murph," he says, wiping off his goggles.

It's a blisteringly cold day, and though the sun shines, I haven't felt my toes in several runs. I wonder if we can go inside and warm up, and maybe get some hot chocolate in the lodge and sit by the fire. I ask Dad if we can, and he says I should ask Mom, but she and Marnie are still making their way down the mountain in their careful snowplows. They don't like skiing as much as we do.

Mom likes to ski if she is the only person on the mountain, but if anyone skis close, she freaks out and yells embarrassing things at them, like "You got mashed potatoes for brains!" The kids on the mountain call her "Mashed Potato Lady."

Mom and Marnie join us at the lift, and I ask Mom if we can go get hot chocolate. She says we cannot, and I tell her I am very cold. She says we cannot, once more, and I whine a little, after which she becomes frighteningly quiet.

We scoot into the lift line, and Mom slides up next to me.

"I'll be taking Erin up," she says to Dad.

Uh oh.

When we get to the lift, Mom and I get on together and she says nothing for a few minutes as we gaze out onto the hill. Skiers swish by beneath us at various speeds, and I think for just a bit that everything will be okay. But it is not okay.

"You know, Erin," says Mom, somewhat menacingly. "All you ever do is bitch. You bitch, bitch, bitch..."

And then Mom gets caught in a kind of "bitch loop," which is exactly what you think it is—the repeating of the word "bitch" again and again—except that there's a kind of building quality to it, which means that once Mom has said about six bitches, she escalates it and takes it up another a notch in volume and tone. Halfway up the hill, her bitches are quite audible from all directions, and the lady on the lift in front of us turns around to see what's going on.

As we near the top of the lift, she's yelling it now, and the word "bitch" has really left the station in terms of context and meaning because it doesn't really sound like a verb anymore.

"BITCH, BITCH, BITCH!"

It gets long and drawn out the louder it gets, and then finally slows into one last, elongated purge of:

"*BIIIIIIIIIIIIIIIIIIIIIIIIITCH.*"

Mom takes a couple deep breaths and then casually lifts the safety bar. She slides down the little hill at the top of the lift and skates out of the way. She adjusts her white hat and smooths her ski suit, slips her goggles over her eyes, and straps on her poles.

When Dad and Marnie get off the lift, Dad skates over to Mom and asks her if she's okay.

"Oh, I'm fine," she says, and then the three of them skate away. I swallow.

My stomach hurts.

⪥

I'm home from school again, alone. It's wintertime, and dark in the house. There's an itch inside me, and I don't how to reach it.

I go into the den and fart around a little bit. There are notes about meetings and reports on Dad's desk, little bits of information I can't understand. His handwriting is block print that slants dramatically with big swooping tails and powerful ascenders. I pick up a pen and practice writing like him. I write my name like he would.

I wander around a little and then head upstairs.

His bedroom is dark and cold. I smell all his colognes. I run my hand down his shirts in his closet. He likes a lot of starch.

There's some dirty laundry on the closet floor. I lie down on it and close the door.

⪥

He isn't going to slip past me this time. I'm going to wake early, and I am going to be in the kitchen when he leaves for the woods, and we are going to go cross-country skiing together, and I will make him see me. He doesn't have to work today, so he can't say, "I have to work." He won't be tinkering in the basement on one of his projects so he can't say "I'm busy." It's too early for his late night games of *Minesweeper* or solitaire on the computer, or the reading of one of his stupid books about spies or elite special forces soldiers who defuse nuclear missiles and save the world so they can bang lots of hot chicks.

And I have been clever, and gotten up early so he can't slip past me and head out into the woods alone. Today his time is for me and I will make him see me.

He smiles as he greets me in the kitchen, the smile with the half-moon eyes. It doesn't feel terribly genuine. I've caught him off guard being the quiet, clever girl who has woken up early and dressed in the dark—normal underwear, long underwear, ski pants, turtleneck, and gaiters.

He makes a thermos of hot cocoa for us while I jibber jabber, and then Dad loads our skis into the back of the station wagon. We drive out to the country and park on the side of the road. Dad gets out and pulls the skis and poles from the back, and I clip the toes of my boots into the bindings of my skis. He floats down into the forest on a cloud of fresh powder and I float down after him.

I slide along in Dad's tracks, chirping about anything that comes to mind, because I have been the cleverest girl and now I get to talk to him. He says nothing back, but I get to talk to him and I can say whatever I want, and when I want to hear his voice to know he is there—with me, and *only* me—I can simply ask him questions. I don't care that he answers them in one- or two-word sentences or fragments.

We ski many miles into the forest this way. Sometimes, I am silent as we ski because Dad is much better than me, his strides are much longer, and it is hard to keep up.

When we reach the end of the trail—a clearing in the woods—

Dad unclips his bindings and steps out of his skis. He takes out the cocoa and fills a little wax paper cup for each of us. We take our mittens off and sit on a log a little while enjoying the cocoa, and the forest, which is full of flakes now. Dad swats my leg playfully with his mitten and smiles. I decide I will say it now.

"Mom is mean," I blurt. "She's mean."

Dad says nothing. My throat swells with anxiety, and my heart races.

I double down. Maybe he doesn't know? I just have to tell him and then he will know and he can help me.

"Mom is mean," I say again. "And it hurts."

But Dad says nothing again. He roots through his backpack and pulls out a hanky. He blows his nose into it and puts it away again. I crumple my cup and place it in his palm and he stows this too in his backpack.

The he stands and puts his mittens on, and finally he speaks.

"Your mom can be very mean," he says.

Oh my god, I think. *Is this happening? Could this be happening?*

I feel a rush of something wonderful fill my body, and my face lights up in a grin. I have been the cleverest girl, waking early, and I have figured out a way to make him see me.

"I worry," says Dad, bending down to clip his boots into his bindings.

YOU DO?

Oh my God, what is happening?

"You do?" I ask. I'm breathless. *This can't be real.*

"Yes," says Dad, straightening his hat and strapping into his poles. "Your mother can be so mean to Marnie."

I run down the aisle to the cockpit, and I find that both pilots are dead, slumped over in their seats for a reason I don't know. I jiggle the little joystick that steers the plane, which looks like an Atari joystick, and it flops back and forth with no effect on the plane.

I press buttons on the console, but nothing happens. I slap the console, pressing all the buttons at once, but the plane doesn't move, and the mountains grow bigger as we sink.

I turn around and see a note tacked to the cockpit door:

Dear Murph, I took all the parts out of the plane. Love, Dad.

I see my sister and mother in the back of the plane and call out to them. "We have to land the plane!" I say, but they don't seem to hear me.

I run back to them and flap my arms over my head. "Mom! Marnie!" I say. "Wake up!" They're each holding a dolly with yellow hair, brushing and smoothing in a trance.

I run back to the cockpit of the plane. There's a mountain dead ahead and it's getting bigger. I jiggle the joystick, but nothing happens.

The mountain is mere feet from the nose of the plane.

Dr. Granger finally gets very angry with me during a Tuesday session on a bright winter day, at one point standing and stomping her bony feet about her office in frustration, speaking to me in what's close to a yell and then decompressing against the cold of her picture window.

I feel badly that I've irked her so much, but I can't lie to her, either. The problem is me. It *has* to be me.

She tells me she is failing me, and I say she is not. I like coming to see her and I need her help. We can figure this out.

Then Dr. Granger puts her head in her hands, sighs sadly, and sits in silence for a spell.

"You know my website is really awful," she says.

❀ ❀ ❀

I design Dr. Granger two websites, business cards and letterhead, and several dozen graphics packages for her speaking tours—flyers, slide decks, email announcements, etc.—during our now thrice weekly therapy sessions I cannot afford, and do not enjoy. I don't know why I do it, and can't seem to say no to her when she asks.

When we don't discuss the many graphic ways that I can assist Dr. Granger with her career during our sessions, we discuss what I can do to lose the immense amount of weight I didn't know I needed to lose so that I can become what Dr. Granger calls "a success," or thin as a wisp with an Anna Wintour-type bob haircut. When we don't discuss that, we discuss what kind of makeup I ought to buy and wear every day to make my face tolerable for rich men to look at. She sits with me at my computer researching wrap dresses with high slits and deep necklines. "Get out your credit card," she says, finally finding the one she likes best.

Sometimes we talk about the plastic surgery and cosmetic procedures she buys with my money, and I try to hold down my lunch as she goes into gory detail about syringes full of fillers and the cutting and hoisting of her facial skin.

One day she begins to tell me dramatic stories from her childhood. She says I'll appreciate them because I am a writer. She tells me about her abusive mother, and how hard it was to be her daughter, and she tells me of her distant father, and how he was never there for her.

"Are you taking notes?" she asks me, and I am confused about why I should do such a thing. "For the book you're going to write about me," she says. When I ask why I would write a book about her she says "Because I am the only strong voice in your life, silly goose."

Dr. Granger is the expert, I say to myself. I guess I could write a book about her.

YOU SHOULD BE GLAD SHE EVEN SPEAKS TO YOU, ERIN.

One horrendous book later, Dr. Granger says we should celebrate. She says now is the time for me to use all my publishing design connections to get a book deal for us. I don't want to say this to her—because she's like a mother to me—but no one would ever publish this book. It reads like someone scavenged the trash in the writers' room on set at *General Hospital*.

I tell her I am very sorry, but I don't think I should try to publish it. Dr. Granger becomes angry with me, and for a time only speaks of her problems with her other patients, people she has a much closer relationship with than me. "They really love me," she says. "They're making such great progress." When I speak of what's going on in my own life, she says, "Get over it."

Many times I leave our sessions and burst into tears, and at one point, I consider seeing a therapist to help me with my other therapist. I don't understand why Dr. Granger has abandoned me, but I think it must be something having to do with me being a bad patient.

One night I catch myself thinking about Dr. Granger in a very familiar way—*I need to try harder to be the perfect patient*—and there's no way of dancing around this fact:

MY RELATIONSHIP WITH THIS WOMAN IS A RECREATION OF SOME RELATIONSHIP I'VE ALREADY HAD.

I leash Murph and head out into the night for a head-clearing walk, upon which I have *another* of my rare rational thoughts:

MAYBE DR. GRANGER IS JUST AN ASSHOLE?

☻ ☻ ☻

It's taken a lot of pep talks and rehearsals for me to summon the strength to do this, but I simply have no choice. Dr. Granger is poison and I need her out of my life, if for no other reason than I'm broke as fuck and no longer have the funds to pay her to talk about herself. I have no idea that this decision will finally lead to me getting what I've wanted from Dr. Granger all along.

I tell her frankly that I need to leave treatment, and Dr. Granger finally gives me the diagnosis I've been longing for all this time. She says she's been keeping it a secret up until now, because she cares so much about me and doesn't want to hurt my feelings, but the truth of the matter is, I am correct. I have severe mental problems and I need to be on medicines right this instant. For me to leave treatment would be disastrous.

But it's way too late in the game for Granger to pull this move. I'm not the brightest bulb in the tanning bed, but even I know she's full of shit.

I ask her what my proper diagnosis is, and she tells me that it is basically everything. I'm psychotic, bipolar, and a sociopath. I'm schizophrenic too. I can't leave because that's just my "avoidance" or whatever. I can't go anywhere. I can't live without her.

But I know this isn't true, because in getting to know Dr. Granger, I have begun to realize that I have *never* needed a drug in my life.

What I have needed all along is to not be the drug some other person consumes to deal with their own crippling inability to feel whole. I need to not be crushed and snorted like a thing without feelings and I need all people like Dr. Granger to go away from me.

When I do not show for my next session, Dr. Granger leaves desperate voicemails for me that I do not answer. Murph and I go to stay with a friend for a few days so that I can clear my head.

Dr. Granger looks up the phone numbers of friends whose names I've mentioned during our therapy sessions and she informs them that they should try to contact me immediately, which they do in various states of panic. Dr. Granger has told them I am on illicit drugs, and that I am out of control and I might try to kill myself. Dr. Granger tells them the police have found my car in the desert with blood in it, and I am nowhere to be found.

Dr. Granger coerces a friend of mine to do an illegal cell tower ping to pinpoint my location.

"I'm fine," I say from the road. "Dr. Granger is nuts."

When I arrive at my friend's apartment, I open up my computer to check my email and see what it is that Dr. Granger wants so badly. At first, her messages are about me being mentally ill and needing her help. When these messages are not answered, she begins to tell me I am headed for doom in various, almost *General Hospital*-like ways. After these go unanswered, she enters a guilt phase, and reminds me how much she has done for me, and then finally she tells me what she wants from me:

The login and password of her website hosting account.

When I return to Arizona, my landlord tells me that someone has broken into my apartment and taken nothing.

Dr. Granger is my last "Erin Type" relationship.

Actual Size	☐ Normal

Emotional Size	■ Slightly Off
	▨ Messed Up
	▦ Fucked In The Head
	▨ Not Long for This World

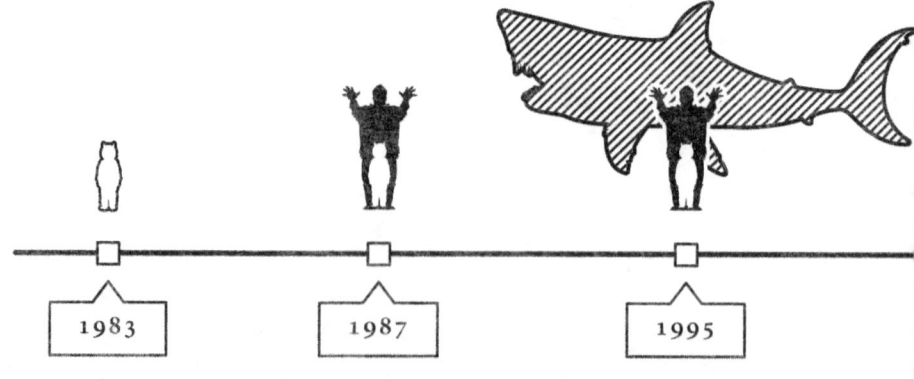

1983   1987   1995

As I near the end of
my time in Arizona...

...it becomes more difficult to stay bottled up. My time with Granger has been eye-opening, to say the least, and I'm beginning to ask questions that are causing a seismic shift in me.

And at the worst possible time, my family comes to visit.

THE WAVE

A dream

I am standing on the screened-in porch of our old home in Fulton, New York, looking out the window. There is a black tidal wave hundreds of feet tall, ripping toward our house and destroying everything it touches.

I'm going to die. It is coming to kill me.

I run into the living room and find my mother vacuuming the carpet in a tank and running shorts, her blonde hair held back with her red cleaning bandana. "Ma!" I say. I shake her shoulders. "Ma! We have to go! There's a wave coming. We're going to die!"

She looks down and starts vacuuming again.

I run back to the porch. The wave is closer now and it seems a mile high.

"Ma, come with me!" I scream, as I run out the back door and up a hill behind the house, stumbling in the thick grass.

I scramble to the top of the hill, and just as I turn around, I see the wave crash onto the hillside and then rip back down, stripping everything away.

Our house is gone. My mother is gone.

My family has been nice to me all day, which is quite confusing. We go for a jeep tour to vistas, a few light hikes, and shopping for magical crystals that are supposed to imbue us with different healing energies. We get tarot card readings from a nice trans lady with press-on nails. She tells me that all is right in my life, and apart from not drinking the correct water—a magical, PH-balanced water I can buy from the health food store—*all is right in my world*.

Even then, I chuckle at the irony.

Now we are at a Mexican restaurant having dinner, and things have soured.

There is a detectable, almost visible, energy between my parents that I have seen before, a tension that can be interpreted as: "Now is the time for the 'Erin Correction' we discussed back in New York." It shouldn't be long before I'm told that they are "terribly worried" about me, and that my life—in its current state—is "troubling," which is the word they use not to describe their concern for me, but more the sting of social embarrassment their shitbird friends subject them to when they hear I am unmarried, broke, and living in a new age mecca full of artists, psychics, and healers in Bumfuck Arizona, which isn't what they would do. Which makes it wrong, apparently.

It doesn't bother me that they've never had an original thought, and lived meaning-free lives built on the fine art of blaming others and material good (toy) worship. *Why should it bother them that I'm broke and weird?*

THE WAVE

Just the thought of such a conversation exhausts me, and I know it is coming.

My mother is in the bathroom when the waiter brings us our margaritas. My father, Marnie, and I had all ordered regulars, and Mom had ordered a peach one. The waiter sets the peach drink in front of me, and my regular margarita at Mom's chair, and because I need the sweet relief of liquor, I suck Mom's peach margarita into me at just shy of brain freeze speed. My esophagus is quite cold. It is gone, and I am slurping the last bits of it through my straw when Mom returns from the restroom.

She sits down to her seat at the table and sees that her margarita is incorrect, and that the residue in my now empty glass is peachy colored.

"Why did you take my margarita?" she asks, with a grave sincerity.

"Wait, what?" I ask.

"You drank my margarita," she says. There is an air of menace in her voice.

I explain that I did not know it was her peach margarita—the waiter had set it down and I had consumed it.

At this point, there is an added tinge to the energy between my parents, who glance back and forth at each other and make judgmental faces. This could be the opening they are looking for, or it could be symbolic of the bigger picture, which is the one of me being born and then being a drain on their finances, emotions, and overall well-being as human beings since the day I stabbed my way out of my mother, both late and too early on the worst day of the worst blizzard in modern history. Or they could simply be concerned by how much I drink. Admittedly, I drink a lot more than I *should*.

It's the first option, it turns out, because "Erin Correction" begins shortly after the waiter brings another round of margaritas, apologizes for the mix-up and drops a red plastic basket full of chips to our table.

I am a mixture of fear and frustration. My jaw is tight, and my molars grind against each other. If I'm being honest, I want to go over the table and throttle my mother. I want to pour peach margarita down her throat until she chokes, and laugh at her and say, "Is this enough? Huh? Is this ENOUGH?" This is not my finest moment as a human being.

They are so worried about me, they say.

I look at Marnie. She takes tiny bites from a chip, gazing blankly at a portrait of a mariachi on the wall. *Are you kidding me, Marnie? Am I not your sister, Marnie?*

My life has no purpose or direction. I'm not married, and I don't have children, though noone ever asked me if I wanted to have them. I have no money and I live in this strange town full of strange people who do things that could never be bragged about at dinner parties, or at that Swedish Fish Lodge thingy they belong to, or at the annual neighborhood Super Bowl party when everybody they know comes over, eats pizza and seven-layer dip, and measures their children against each other to create a parent-performance hierarchy my parents will never find themselves at the top of, because: *me*.

I nod, sympathetically, and inwardly, *I seethe*.

I am so very tired of living only for their emotional needs, and I don't think I can do it anymore. There's something very big and dark in me that I hold back, and playing this dumb game year after year—the game of them being so close to happy if only I weren't *Erin*—whittles away at my ability to do it. I know it's coming some day soon. I don't know that day is today. The moment is now, because they ask me not to write.

The writing, they say. It is a problem. And I write about things you simply shouldn't write about, let alone post online for everyone to see—for their peers to see, and to snicker at behind my parents' backs like spineless twats.

I take deep breaths and try to understand where they're coming from. It's true, I write about some taboo stuff. I suppose I could always take it down a notch. I tell them I will try to dial it back a little, which is not enough, apparently.

"What would your grandmother think?" asks my father, and I am dumbfounded.

I dig my fork into my leg and grind my teeth in an attempt to keep from saying exactly what I end up saying, which is:

"Honestly Dad, I don't give a *fuck*."

My father's face cringes and purses. "Nice mouth," he says. *Nice mouth?* Mom says I'm "disgusting."

I try to breathe. I try to be rational, but I might be breaking.

Oh, that is very definitely a cracking sound, I know it. Does anyone else hear that?

I make one last push for peace, composing myself and going back in, this time with the brutal truth Granger always told me I needed to give them. I *cannot* love this imbecilic character they've written for me, and they cannot accept me as I really am. Our relationship will break me if it stays on this course, and if they do not already know this, then I will them them right now.

I say…words.

I wish I could recall what they were, the tone I used and where all the pregnant pauses went, but the truth is, it came flying out of me like vomit in an explosive, heart-felt whoosh of personal truth, during which I got a little dizzy and might have almost cried.

The gist of it was this: I hated the person they wanted me to be, and I had tried to die at least once—maybe twice—but not long after that, I discovered writing, and it is probably the only reason I'm still alive aside from my sweet Murph. If I gave it up, it would break me.

That's tangential, they say. Stop being dramatic, they say. I cannot write anymore because it embarrasses them. But really, I know they mean to say this: I have no business being the writer of my own story.

I tell my family they can't be in my life any longer, not if I'm ever going to figure out how to like myself.

And, subsequently, every feeling I've refused to feel during the last twenty years comes crashing down upon me.

I CRY... A LOT.

(Feeling is not weakness. It is strength).

THE BAD ONE
PART THREE
self

It's been ten years since
Mark died.

I become obsessed. Sometimes I write two or three times a day. I log whole books on my Mac, chronicling anything that comes up, and anything I've ever refused to feel, pushed down or run from.

I discover that writing about my teenage years is especially difficult.

Progress is *painful*.

It isn't a suggestion anymore. They don't act it out in symbolism or in the tiny bit of a disparity in the respective levels of warmth they dole out to Marnie and me.

They come right out and say it now; *they do not like me.*

They mock me. They make fun of my face and my body. They mock my "weird" opinions—which are wrong opinions because they're *different* opinions—and then they laugh at me for feeling sad or upset when I am mocked, because it's all *just jokes*. I need to get a sense of humor.

That's another thing that's wrong with me.

They poke fun at the most minute of things, like the way my arms hang when I walk through the house or the way I lip sync along to songs I like on the radio. They sarcastically repeat the things I say, so that I know for sure that the things I say are ridiculous, and though most fathers think *no boy is ever good enough* for their daughters, my father thinks *all boys are too good for me.* "Run!" he tells boys, when they come to see me at the house.

"Run away, har har."

I cry in my bedroom and they tell me to shut up. I'm being too loud; they're trying to read.

And everything bad that happens to them is my fault. Life would be so much easier if it weren't for Erin, the worst kid ever who gets straight A's and zero detentions.

They tell stories at cookouts and dinner parties about what

a pain in the ass I am because I pooped and the toilet overflowed, and I ate the chicken we were supposed to take on the picnic the next day, and I forgot to tell them about my softball game, and I fell down the hill at the Fenton Historical Center in my brand-new pink stretch pants and tore a hole in the knee. I cost them stretch pants and I cost them co-pays and one time—*can you believe it*—I poured too much vanilla extract onto the cookie dough, and I ruined the goddamn Christmas cookies.

Sometimes the mocking doesn't even *make sense*.

Dad buys a new station wagon that turns out to be a lemon, and it needs so much maintenance it nearly bankrupts us; it's Erin's fault because "Erin liked the color." Marnie T-bones a lady in that station wagon, and it's Erin's fault because "her head was in the way." When Mom's mood sours and she has her outbursts for a reason she can't explain, the reason becomes me—I burned pancakes and now the house smells, or I got a B in science when her friends' kids got A's, or I moved her nippers from the nipper spot where they should be kept at just the right nipper angle, or I read her *People Magazine*, or I played my INXS tape too loudly on the stereo and danced around to it like goddamn weirdo.

Or I just *am*. I exist. And I am *not them*.

I hate myself more with each passing day, and I don't understand why any of this is happening. I'm still a child, and I don't know what scapegoating is. Hell, I won't know what it is until I'm in my thirties, when Granger tells me about African witch children during one of our sessions. I'm being cut down a millimeter at a time—soul death by vegetable peeler.

I begin to eat junk food in secret for a reason I don't understand. I wait until everyone goes to bed, and then I sneak back down and eat myself sick. I'm getting fat, and Mom is very angry about it. I know I need to stop, but I can't seem to do it.

☠ ☠ ☠

There's a winter formal coming up, and I can't get a date to it. I'm fat now, and the boys don't like me anymore.

Getting fat is rather ironic in that, while the size of me is expanding, I'm becoming more invisible every day. The fatter I get, the less people see me. The world has decided I am fat and thus a nothing person—no longer pleasing to look upon, so I do not count.

Mom has been pushing me to lose weight. She says if I do, she will buy me a beautiful dress for the formal. I have been going to aerobics classes at the YMCA, but I haven't lost a pound because I can't stop eating.

Mom asks me every day if I have a date for the formal, and every day I have to let her down and say, "No." I am fat, and boys don't like me anymore. As the date of the formal is approaching, she tells me to ask a boy to go with me.

I ask several boys to the dance, and they say no, of course, because I am fat. It is absolutely humiliating.

The formal is now a week away, and I have no date to it. My mother comes home from work in a foul mood, and I naively hide from her in my bedroom, thinking I can duck her and her questions altogether.

"Did you find a date to the dance?" asks Mom, letting herself into my room.

"No one will go with me," I say, my face hot from panic. Mom scowls at me.

YOU FUCKING PIG, ERIN.

I lie on my side on my bed with a pillow shoved into my thumping belly. I've been having terrible stomachaches lately for a reason I can't understand.

Mom says she doesn't understand why I don't have a date. "What's so hard about this?" she wonders out loud. "When there's a formal you find a boy to go with you. You dress up and you take pictures. How could this be *so difficult?*"

I start to cry. I don't understand anything in my life right now. "I'm sorry," I say.

GO DROWN YOUR TEARS IN ANOTHER SWISS CAKE ROLL, YOU FUCKING PIG.

Mom paces around my room. She asks me, "What's so hard" about finding a date to a dance; her footfalls are heavy as she paces both because she's angry with me and because her own heft has become weighty as of late.

"What is *wrong* with you?" she asks me, her eyes wide and flat. Her irises are those little green islands in the sea of bloodshot white. I tell her I don't know what's wrong with me, and then I tell her I am sorry again.

She asks me if my best friend, Lindsay, has a date to the dance, and I say that she does. Many boys asked Lindsay to go, because Lindsay is beautiful and thin, with long blonde hair, slim-fit jeans, and creamy, glowing skin. "Why can't you be like Lindsay?" Mom always asks me. Every day I hear it. "Why can't you be like Lindsay?" I don't measure up.

I tell her Lindsay is going to formal with a dreamy Junior boy. I can see her wheels turning as she imagines it, and imagines how lovely the pictures will be. She could really see herself as the mother of a slim blonde who dates junior boys.

BUT SHE'S THE MOTHER OF A WORTHLESS FATTY, ISN'T SHE?

I tell her I am sorry a few more times. I am so sorry I am not someone else, someone better. I'm sorry I am not Lindsay, or anyone she thinks is good and decent.

Mom paces and gesticulates. She demands answers. She's building into one of her loops again, but this one isn't a "bitch loop." It's something different altogether.

She stomps in her heavy circles in my bedroom, gaining speed and tearing at her temple hair. She works herself into a primal holler of, "WHAT THE FUCK IS WRONG WITH YOU?"

She's in full twister mode.

"WHAT THE FUCK IS WRONG WITH YOU? WHAT THE FUCK IS WRONG WITH YOU?"

My stomach is thumping wildly now. It feels like I swallowed a porcupine. I am sobbing, and I have no answer to her question. I don't know why I am so bad and why everything I do is wrong. I don't know why I hurt my family all the time or why I can't stop eating. *I don't know. I don't know. I don't know. anything at all.*

"WHAT THE FUCK IS WRONG WITH YOU? WHAT THE FUCK IS WRONG WITH YOU?"

I hold the pillow to my face and sob.

☙ ☙ ☙

It is summertime and the house is hot. Everyone is in bed for the night and I am watching MTV.

I go to the kitchen for one of my late night binges, and root through the cabinets for something tasty. There's no popcorn, or bread to make toast. There are no more chips and no Swiss cake rolls.

I open the fridge to see what's inside, but nothing looks terribly tasty. I spy a case of beer in the back, and a little voice inside my head says: *Oh, yes please!*

So I pull out a can and crack the top. It smells and tastes like bad breath in liquid form, so I plug my nose and drink it down as fast as I can. When it's empty, I toss the can into the trash and cover it with a paper towel, thinking naively that Mom won't find it.

I head back to the living room and sit down on the sofa. Sinead O'Connor is spinning in circles on the television, and I think she is very pretty. I feel a pleasant warmth in my body, the first pleasantness I have felt there in a long time. I feel invigorated, somehow, and I feel *alive*. I dance around a little bit with Sinead, and when MTV breaks for commercials, I crash back down onto the sofa. The world is beautiful now, and I feel slippery and warm. There is no reason to be sad anymore.

I wonder if I have discovered the secret to happiness. *When you are sad, you drink beer?* It seems easy enough to do.

And if one beer makes me this happy, what would two do? Or even three?

Six carelessly hidden cans of beer later, I am lying on the sofa, and I am not so happy. Metallica is angry on the television.

"DARKNESS, IMPRISONING ME..."

The room begins to spin in circles, and though I close my eyes and grab on to the cushion beneath me, I can't stop the spin. I try to stay very still and quiet, but it soon becomes clear to me that I am going to vomit and it is going to happen very soon.

I run up the stairs to my bedroom, thinking if I go to sleep, everything will be okay. I lie in bed like I did on the sofa, gripping the sheets beneath me to stop the spin, and when I can't hold it in any longer, I sit up straight and beer sprays onto my bedroom wall in three guttural whooshes.

I fall back onto my bed and pass out.

Mom is in the kitchen the next morning, and there are six

empty beer cans carefully placed on the table before her, like evidence in a courtroom trial.

"What's this?" she asks me with the menace voice.

I go straight to lying. I say I don't know, and I've never seen them before. Then Mom asks me why there is beer vomit all over my bedroom wall, and I feel pretty stupid about the lie.

"I did it," I say.

She gets up and hurls the cans back into the trash.

"How do you think this makes *me* look?" asks Mom. "What would my friends think of me if they knew about this?" I don't know what to say. "They'd think I was *trash*, that's what! Is that what you're trying to do? TO MAKE ME LOOK LIKE TRASH?"

I hadn't thought about that at all, actually. I just didn't want to hurt anymore.

She screams at me until she feels better, and then she grounds me for the summer.

    FUCKING TRASH. FUCKING PIG.

☻ ☻ ☻

The Buffalo Bills are playing. Mom and Marnie are in their Bills sweatshirts on the sofa, and I'm on the floor under a tray table drawing trees. Bruce Smith crashes into poor Drew Bledsoe, who crumbles to dust and gives up the ball. There's whooping and celebratory high fives as the Bills go on to win the game.

I pull a pretzel from the communal bowl, pry each salt grain from it with my teeth, and then pop it into my mouth and chew. I am waiting, patiently. I just have to hold on for a little while longer.

Dad creeps up the basement steps in his leather slippers, stopping behind the sofa to pet Soupy, who is perched there. She purrs and flexes her paws in appreciation for the scratches. He's been in the basement all day working on his Dad projects, but now it's time for him to go to bed—after he plays *Minesweeper* or Solitaire on the PC in the upstairs office for an hour.

Mom and Marnie go to bed, too, and then I am alone.

I pop a bag of microwave popcorn and melt extra butter on top. I wash it down with soda, and when it's all gone, I pop another bag, drizzle even more butter on top, and drink more soda until I feel like I may burst.

YOU WORTHLESS PIECE OF SHIT.

Then I go down into the basement, get out the bucket, and poke the back of my throat until everything in my stomach comes out again and I am unburdened. I dump the goop out behind the shed and then I wash it and put it back again. I clean my face and hands in the utility sink, and though my knees scream and my throat aches, I feel much better than I did before.

I feel clean, somehow.

I'm down twenty-five pounds.

☠ ☠ ☠

My legs buzz with a pleasant vibration. I'm tired, of course, but those happy chemicals that come out on a long, cleansing run always make me feel so good about myself. I try to calculate the calories I have burned as I head up the back steps into the house. My new healthy habits have led to a thirty-five-pound weight loss and people are beginning to see me again. Sometimes they even say, "Hey, you look great," and Mom said she was proud of me the other day.

I kick my running shoes off in the mudroom, and go to the kitchen for some water. I find Mom there, sitting unhappily at the kitchen table, scowling as she waves her hand Vanna White–like toward the plastic grocery bag full of last night's vomit I had hid in the trash and thought I would never see again. I am awash with panic.

"What's *this*?" asks Mom with the menace voice.

I don't know what to say, and I don't want to say anything at all. I'm so embarrassed and ashamed I want to run out the back door and never come home again.

"You're disgusting," she says.

I have really let her down this time.

She cannot see herself as the kind of mother who has a daughter like this. What would people think?

I say I am sorry, again and again, and do a little nervous dance in place. I don't *mean* to hurt her like this, I tell her. I don't *mean* to be disgusting.

"You never *mean to*, do you?" she says.

She throws the bag back into the trash and washes her hands with hot water and soap. Disgusting, she says. Gross, she says.

When she's done, she turns around and gets very close to my face. She grabs me by my shoulders. "You're not going to do this again," she says. "Do you hear me?" I nod, yes, I hear her. I won't do it again.

"Good," she says. "It's *such* a waste of food."

It's probably four o'clock, the hour during which the horrible things happen.

It's wintertime and dark already. I am wrapped in three afghans and wear several layers' worth of shirts and fleeces—I never feel warm anymore. I turn the television on and set up a tray table, and then I roll one orange up and down my leg.

It loosens the hide from the fruit. Any expert orange peeler will roll their orange first.

I get out my special peeling tool and carve the hide open, and the smell of orange oil spraying from the peel makes my stomach rumble with anger. I never give it enough. Not anymore. Now I am in charge, and it can whine all it wants, but I will say when we will eat and I will say how much.

I tear the hide from the orange and stack it in a pile at the far end of the paper towel. I suppose this orange is technically edible at this point, if I had low orange-eating standards and no self-control. This isn't eating; this is a game I play. *How long can I go? How much can I take?*

I play a running game too. *How far can I go, how fast can I do it, and how little can I eat beforehand?*

I can't say I know how long it takes to take the veins off. I don't time myself, and I imagine each orange is different, with a different amount of veinage that has to be removed. But I am surgical as I lift the white gunk from the orange sections, carefully stacking it on the paper towel in the corner. When the veins are gone, surely the orange should be eaten. *Shouldn't it?* If I were a gluttonous fatty with no self-control, then yes. But I am *not*, so I take the extra step of removing the outer skin that holds the section together, making a careful incision at the top with the peeler tool and unwrapping the sections until all that remains are the pulpy tubes of pure, sweet juice.

Then, and only then, may I eat this orange.

I haven't had a period in eight months and my hair is falling out. At night, I sandwich myself between two electric blankets to stay warm, and I sleep with a pillow between my thighs and dream about eating whole pints of ice cream.

My thighs haven't touched each other for almost a year.

I weigh 105 pounds, but I'm shooting for 95. It just seems like a nice round number.

And I have never in my life been *so seen*.

My best buddy, Lindsay, enters the Junior Miss Pageant—a scholarship competition open to all the excellent senior girls, countywide—and I am certain that she will win it. I even design a dress for her to wear, a simple red sheath dress with a slit and a scoop neck, and she looks amazing in it.

She will go on to take the crown with ease, but that isn't the important part of this story.

Mom and I go to all out war over the Junior Miss Pageant.

She says I will do it. I absolutely must enter it—she can really see herself as the mother of a Junior Miss. I will enter this pageant and I will do an excellent tap dance for the judges, and I will wear a gown and smile, and be perfect for her in front of all her friends.

In a rare show of spine, I tell her, emphatically, that I will not enter this pageant. I will absolutely, under no circumstances prance around on a stage in a dress and sash, and blather on about world peace. This is *not* who I am, and it would be preposterous for me to pretend otherwise.

She says it *is* who I am.

I say it is *not*.

No, she says. It *is*.

I wonder why we don't just scoop my guts out like a Halloween pumpkin so she can wear me around like a puppet?

She screams and stomps. She goes into several loops. She demands to know how it is—after everything she has done for me—that I can't be bothered to do this one little thing for her.

She never asks me for *anything*, she says, tears in her eyes.

I may not be able to graduate high school in May.

I'm approaching the "automatic failure" number of missed school days. My grades are still good, but if I continue to be out sick at the current rate, I won't make it.

If I can't graduate, I can't pose for pictures with my friends in my cap and gown. Even worse, I can't go to the Senior Celebration Night party that my mother has busted her ass to put together, donating her nights and weekends to petition local businesses for goods and services. She's really put her heart into it, and I don't want to let her down.

I know I can't get sick if I want to get my degree, but I can't really stop myself from being sick, either.

The stomachaches come on for days at a time, now, and when they come, they twist my belly up in spasms the likes of which I have never fully been able to explain any better than saying it's as if someone has driven a train spike through my gut. I lie for hours in cold puddles of sweat on our bathroom tile with spit pooling under my face, because it hurts too much to swallow. I can't move, I can't breathe, and if someone handed me a loaded gun, I'd no doubt pull the trigger to stop the pain.

The doctors don't know what's wrong with me, so they have me drink barium, and they watch it move through my stomach. When they can't find anything suspicious there—no notch or node that looks out of sorts, and no material cause for what ails me—they shrug and say "irritable bowel syndrome?"

Mom begs me to tell her what is wrong with me, and I don't have an answer for her. (I won't have an answer, myself, until I'm in my thirties.)

I'm sick again, lying on the living room sofa. Dad's car pulls into the driveway. Mom is in the kitchen, making dinner. The door opens and then quietly snaps shut again, and Mom says hello in a sad tone.

Graduation is two months away, and I only have a few sick days left.

I can hear my name being said, and I can hear the rumble of low-volume voices having a conversation that's not to be heard.

It's my mother who raises her voice first. "What is wrong with her?" she says, crying. I hear my father trying to comfort her.

"I've worked so hard to make her *perfect*," she says, as if I'm a broken appliance.

I hear my father shush her and imagine he's pulled her in for a hug. I imagine he rubs her back like I have seen him do. "It's okay," he says. "We'll figure it out," he says.

"Why is she doing this to me?" she asks him.

Am I a Zenith TV you can pound on the side of, to snap the picture back into focus?

Dad comes into the living room and asks me how I am. I tell him I don't feel well and had to stay home from school again.

"Listen," he says. "This has to stop."

Has to stop? I'm sixteen and I'm probably dying, and I don't know why.

"Do you hear me?" he asks. I nod, *yes*. It seems like what he wants. "This can't go on," he says. "You're driving your mother crazy."

Some of my favorite memories from my childhood were the times I spent with my father in the woods.

When we were little, Dad would take us hiking and camping. We'd go apple picking and cross country skiing, and we would make campfires out of nothing and build lean-tos when it rained. He would teach us about the different types of trees and show us the tracks the deer made with their little hooves, how they carved trails into the ferns that lined the forest floor with their wandering about, looking for more sumac berries. It was as if the woods was his true home and he was whole there, so that when we went there with him, he was present and his love was full.

The day we found Drip Dry the Evil Newt was one of

those days.

⏪

It isn't until I am done peeing that I realize I have left my pack of TP at home.

"Dad!" I call from the other side of the mossy trunk. "Dad, I forgot my TP."

"Find a leaf!" yells Dad.

I look around for a good wiping leaf, but it has been raining, and the leaves are slick and slimy.

"All the leaves are wet!" I say.

"Then drip-dry!" says Dad.

I snicker a little, and wiggle my bottom before pulling up my trousers and securing the snap and—while readjusting my turtleneck and wool sweater down over my pants—I spy something pink on the forest floor. I bend down to get a closer look and see that the pinkness is a duo of lizards, with little orange spots on their backs. They're the color of strawberry gummy bears, and nearly the same size.

"Dad!" I yell. "Comere!"

Dad walks over and squats down by the lizards. "Well, I'll be," he says. "Efts."

"What's an eft?" coos Marnie, clearly taken with them.

"It's a baby newt," says Dad. "When they're little, they're a bright pink color, and when they get older, they turn green."

Dad gently plucks the leaf the efts stand upon from the forest floor and places it in his big man palm. Neither of the efts moves a muscle. We gaze at them in awe and then beg Dad to keep them as pets.

"I suppose," says Dad. "We'll put them in the old fish tank."

We walk back to the trailhead with the efts. Dad opens up the hatch of our station wagon, pulls an old tin from his camping backpack, and scoots the efts into it. While scraping the mud off my boots so I can get into the station wagon, I spy another newt. This one is much bigger than the efts, and it isn't as pretty. In fact, it's slightly frightening, and I don't want to touch him.

"I found another one!" I say to Dad, who scoops up the newt and adds it to the tin.

We name our newts on the drive home. Marnie decides the efts will be called Kim and Maureen, and I name the bigger newt Drip Dry.

Dad sets up the newt tank in my bedroom with a little water dish, and I collect some leaves, rocks, and sticks from the backyard to make it homey. We scoot the efts and newt into the tank, and they stand as still as statues.

When I return from eating my dinner, the newts have moved a little; Kim and Maureen are huddled together in one corner of the tank, and Drip Dry is perched in the middle on a rock. I bet they're hungry, so I scoop out the handful of Rice Krispies I put in my pocket and dump it into the tank.

The newts stare blankly into space.

The next morning, when I check the tank, the newts haven't moved in the night. I dump more cereal into the tank, but they don't eat it.

Two days pass and nothing happens, so I fill their dish with fresh water. I sing them a song—"Do Ya Think I'm Sexy?" by Rod Stewart—but they don't move. They don't seem to respond to me in any way, really.

A week into newt ownership, I begin to panic and dump half a bag of mini marshmallows onto the now stinky piles of Rice Krispies. Kim and Maureen stay on one side of the tank, and Drip Dry perches in the middle.

One day I come home from school and Kim and Maureen are no longer in the tank. Drip Dry is still in the tank, and he has become strangely fat in the night—probably from eating marshmallows.

I run screaming through the house for my mother. Has she seen Kim or Maureen?

"I bet they escaped," she says.

I run to the phone and dial Dad at work. I can barely get the words out, I am crying so hard. "Kim and Maureen are gone," I say. "And Drip Dry is fat." My mother grabs the phone from me and says, "Kim and Maureen have escaped from the tank, Dear," and then she hands the phone back to me.

"They must have climbed out," says Dad. "I'm sure they're having a grand old time somewhere in the house."

Mom hands me a flashlight from the junk drawer and wishes me luck. I scour the house looking for them—under every bed and couch, on top of every shelf, inside all the cupboards and the drawers and even in the toilet.

When Dad comes home from work, we decide to set Drip Dry free out behind the woodpile. We say farewell, and head inside for dinner.

For years, I imagine that Kim and Maureen still live with us somewhere in the house, hiding in the various nooks and crannies. I imagine they watch *General Hospital* with us from the blades of the ceiling fan, their little pink chins propped on balled-up, three-toed fists.

But no, the truth is, without even the slightest consideration we might be doing it, we fed Kim and Maureen to Drip Dry.

With graduation a month away, we go back to the hospital and the doctors order another test. They have me fast for two days, take laxatives, and stick suppositories into my ass.

On the day of the test, I take a half-day and leave school early to drive to the radiology center.

The nurses have me strip down and dress me in a thin smock that has an opening in the back, before they take me to a dark room with a metal table in the middle, a large machine next to the table, and monitors above it.

They have me lay on the metal, which is so cold I shake, and a man comes in dressed in medical garb and a mask. "It's all okay," he says, his deep voice comforting.

He places a tube coated in jelly up my ass and tells me I will feel some "cold pressure" in a casual tone. Then liters of ice-cold explosives are pumped into my colon, my belly spasms, and I squeal and rock back and forth, pounding my fists into the metal table.

"You're okay," the man says. "It's okay."

My innards are on display on the monitor above us, and I expect him to look at them and say, "There it is. That's the cause," but he does not. Instead he says, "Everything looks perfect."

The nurses take me to a metal toilet, and I sit on it and spray the liters of barium back out.

The ladies give me orange juice I drink and then puke down the front of my ski jacket while driving myself home.

The doctor told my mother there was nothing physically wrong with me. "I'd recommend you try talk therapy," he said to her, in the gentlest tone he could manage. At this my mother protested, because only crazy people go to therapy, and we are not a crazy family; we're perfect.

But now we're at the office of my first official therapist—a nice lady with a soft round face, who practices from a building downtown—and we're sitting next to each other on the pastel-colored sofa in her treatment room, because Mom was too paranoid to let me talk to this therapist without her.

The lady asks me a few questions about myself, why I have come to see her and such. I answer her in one- or two-word sentences because I am nervous, and my mother interjects every so often, to correct my answers when they are wrong.

At a certain point, the therapist seems more interested in what my mother has to say, and I take a back seat and listen to the two of them talk about my mother's life.

She asks my mother how she feels about all my problems.

My mother takes a tissue from the box and dabs the corners of her eyes where wetness has arisen. She composes herself a little and then tells the lady that she works very hard to be a perfect mother—which is all she ever wanted to be—and no matter how hard she tries to mother me, she just can't seem to fix me.

"That must be hard," the lady says.

"It is," says my mother, blowing her nose into the tissue.

She tells us about her stress at work, and she tells us how overwhelming and out of control her life feels, that her moods are unpredictable and she really struggles. She gets so sad sometimes she feels her heart might break.

I feel a little bit of a lump in my throat.

She talks about the communication problems in her marriage and how her husband is not open with his feelings. She says her parents were alcoholics, and that they were traumatized by the Depression and the war. They fought with each other, bitterly, and Grandpa gambled too much, but they didn't have therapists back then so they drank to manage it.

She says her father only told her that he loved her once, the day President Kennedy was murdered in Dallas. She came home from school early and found him sitting on the couch in a stupor. "I love you, Cindy," he said, and then he never said it again.

She says her father died when she was only twenty-seven. I am crying, now. I put my hand on her knee.

The nice lady reaches for the tissue box, pulls one out, and hands it over. My mother dabs her eyes and blows her nose again. "It feels so good to talk about this," she says.

Our hour ends, and Mom writes a check for the session. Mom says she doesn't feel like going back to work today, so we walk across the street to a convenience store for Snickers bars. We eat them on a bench outside the medical building in the sun. I ask Mom why she never told me all that stuff.

"I don't know," she says. "I was taught you don't talk about things like that."

We drive home in silence, listening along to the radio. At one point Mom says she thinks the session was a success.

"I hope it fixed you," she says.

It won't be long until I am drinking Rumple Minze at a party. I'll get hit by a car, wreck my knee on a bridge, and take a bag full of pills with a half bottle of whiskey, so no, it definitely did not fix me.

But my mother never seemed so human to me as she did inside that room, and really, that's all I ever wanted her to be. I had never been that interested or invested in her Barbie act. To me, she was at her best a little disheveled in her bathrobe with coffee breath, pranking the Department of Public Works and snort laughing.

First I cut everyone from
my life who ever came between
me and *my self*.

After that I wrote my guts out, determined what it was that I felt, and then honored every bit of it. Writing and feeling were practically the same activity.

There came a day I realized I didn't have much more to write about, but I still didn't like myself that much.

I knew I had to do something.

At first I feel sorry for myself.

I drink a lot. I black out in public.

I have nightmares about the world ending, about towers collapsing, about being devoured and about waking up at the center of the earth, a thousand miles from the air I need to breathe at the surface.

I write a lot and I cry a lot—big snotty, guttural tears like I used to cry when I was a kid, the kind of tears that seize up every muscle in your body and freeze your face into a sort of gaping expression of anguish.

I go at heavy bags for hours, till my elbows and shins bleed.

I become one with my anger, and I rant and scream. I wonder how anyone could have made me feel so badly.

Lindsay has a look of terror on her face. "Murph!" she says. "Don't do it! It's much too far."

I look out at the lake. The forty-person amoeba of teenaged arms and legs is now kicking its way across, and the yacht club dock is still jiggling from their initial dive into the water for the annual Chautauqua Institution Yacht Club Swim Across the Lake, circa 1986.

Lindsay is usually right about stuff, and I should probably listen to her. But I won't. I'd rather do it than wonder if it could be done.

I tell the counselors I want to do it too. They don't want to spend the next few hours following me over in a canoe, so they try to talk me out of it.

"You sure?" they ask. "It's pretty far. Wouldn't you rather go make lanyards?"

Like a little baby?

"No," I say. "You don't have to go with me, but I'm going."

Lindsay follows me down the dock, trying to convince me not to go. "It's so far," she says, her brow furrowed. "I'm so worried." I tell her if I wear a life vest it would be cheating. "I'll be fine," I say, and then I plug my nose and jump into the lake.

And then little by little, in a steady breaststroke, I swim across that damn lake.

Lindsay has a very fancy grandma named Mary who lives in fine houses and has fine summer homes. One of Mary's rich husbands left her a cottage on Lake Chautauqua in Chautauqua Institution. It's a mansion to me, nearly twice the size of my house, and furnished in all sorts of rich people décor, and every summer Lindsay and I spend a few weeks there making crafts at the school of art—ceramic pots and collages—or swimming with the teenagers at the yacht club.

The cottage sits on the eastern shores of Chautauqua Institution, with hedgerows and little statues at the front entrance and a dock and tiny beachfront out back.

Lindsay and I like to put our old tennis shoes on and dig for glass in the lake, which is infested with the sharp shells of zebra mussels. Sometimes we find vintage glass under the old drainpipe that carries rainwater out of the Institution, and we use it to build elaborate little castle cities in the sand. Our castles have moats and turrets made of dried leaves. They have portcullises made of Popsicle sticks and fly the colors of whatever ribbons we can find lying around, or the feathers we find on the shore. We make up stories about the people who live there, and sometimes our little cities go to war with one another.

Most of the time the rainwater drips from the drainpipe, but sometimes it comes in great gushes and mows down everything we make.

Later I learn that this pipe used to carry wastewater during the Victorian times, and before the Institution was outfitted with modern plumbing, it carried the piss and shit of rich people, dignitaries, and nobles out of the city and into Lake Chautauqua. Obviously, we never actually played in anyone's waste, as it had been a hundred years' time since they dumped such muck into the lake, but it still grosses me out a little bit when I think about it.

I try to remember all the impressive things that Lindsay and I were able to make out of some glass, some sticks, and some old Victorian shit mud.

How could they make me feel that way?

It's a thought I get locked in for almost a year.

I stomp around town, kicking rocks and screaming into canyons. I take peyote and howl at the moon. I go for long hikes to the magical spots at which humans have been groping for answers for thousands of years, and it's on one of these afternoon journeys in the armpit of Arizona summer heat that I sit on a rock, look out at the horizon, and say:

ERIN, IT'S TIME TO BE HONEST. NO ONE HAS EVER FORCED YOU TO FEEL A THING.

If people in my life ever succeeded in making me hate myself, it was only because I allowed it to happen. They were mean to me, and I colluded with them. We teamed up to bully me, and when I got older, I got caught in a loop of incorrect belief, and then I beat myself up twice as hard as anyone had ever intended.

My biggest enemy in life had been me all along.

It's an ugly and brutal truth, but it leaves me in a powerful position.

If I can *unmake* myself, then I can damn well *remake* myself, and maybe that self can be someone I love.

I'll simply go little by little, in a steady breaststroke. *Why not? I'm a maker. I can make anything. I can make castles out of shit.*

I'd rather do it than wonder if it can be done.

This becomes my mantra. SueEllen giggles when she hears me say it. "Clearly, it must be done," I say.

I have spent my life hating myself with gusto, so it stands to reason, then, that I can use that gusto to love myself. I simply have to make it my new mission. I need to heal myself. I need to be open to trying new things.

And what better place to get *weird* with your healing?

I write and take walks. I stop eating grain. I stop eating sugar, vegetable oil, and processed foods. I spend hours on vibrating tables with needles in my skin, trying to waken my energetic pathways. I lie on SueEllen's treatment table under a haze of sage as she works her magic on my clogged belly, bringing my chakras back to life. I try Reiki; I try crystals. I draw the line at cults and that creepy guy who channels God and then shoves scissors up your nose, but anything else I can get my hands on that could be considered a method of healing is fair game.

Do I believe in all of these methods? *Not really.*

Do they help me feel better? *Absolutely.*

I use mental exercises to forge empathy for myself. When I look back and side with someone other than me, I imagine it all happening to Murph, and then it becomes wildly inexcusable. *Oh my God, how dare they!*

I use mental exercises to quiet the negative voices in my head, which ends up being a trial I am not prepared for. The two sides of me go to all-out war.

ERIN, YOU'RE A DIPSHIT.

YOU SHUT THE FUCK UP!

ERIN, YOU'VE LOST YOUR MIND.

YOU GET THE FUCK OUT OF US, RIGHT THIS INSTANT!

My negative thoughts aren't welcome anymore and I tell them to go away when I notice them rising up. Sometimes, I have to say it twenty times or more a day, and sometimes, I have to say it out loud, in public, in line at the bank or walking through the aisles of the supermarket.

"You shut the fuck up!" I say at the specialty cheeses bin. "You will not speak to us this way," I say by the gluten-free pastas. "We are most certainly *NOT* a bag of shit!" I say as I place my items on the belt.

People are frightened by my behavior, but I don't have the energy to be embarrassed by it. Besides, it's Arizona, the craziest state in the country.

I go for long hikes in the sunshine, up switchbacks, through brush. I lie and soak up the vitamin D, and I meditate and chant mantras. I buy a pack of Louise Hay's positive affirmation cards, pull one every morning, and spend the day soothing myself with it. I practice deep breathing, and take ice-cold showers.

I do a forty-day green juice fast to cleanse my body. My

organs spit out black sludge that smells like what I imagine toxic waste smells like, if you added a few squirts of the expensive perfumes I used to wear in the nineties.

I take spirulina. I take chlorophyll. I take vitamins A, B(s), C, D, E, and K. I take green coffee, selenium, zinc, and potassium. I take Reishi mushroom extract, MSM, bee pollen, glutamine, glutathione, arginine, milk thistle, kava kava, oregano oil, turmeric, elderberry, quercetin, melatonin, probiotics, prebiotics, and roots. I take so many roots I fear I may sprout. I drink teas. I take oils. I pull oils through my teeth to rid my body of toxins. I shoot Kona up my ass. I squirt saline in my nose, and I drink whole pounds worth of organic vegetable juice a day.

I roll out, and I plank. I push-up, and I burpee. I massage, and I exfoliate. I stretch, and I pose. I strengthen. I salt scrub. I sweat. I slather. I rest. I relax, and then I do it all over again, because clearly it must be done.

I'm getting *strong*.

And one day I realize I haven't heard from **THIS VOICE** in a really long time.

Huh.

SueEllen's office is full of dream catchers and crystals. It smells like the sage burning in a shell on her desk. Native flute music plays from a stereo in the corner.

I always feel at peace here. I lived here for a month the

summer prior, while she and her husband took a road trip to the northeast with their dog, Scruffy, and I never slept better in my life.

SueEllen has me sit on her table, and asks me about my life. I say I'm doing well. I haven't noticed "the voice" in a while, so all the work I'm doing to quiet it is really starting to pan out.

"Aren't you a miracle!" she chuckles.

She has me lie back and then she holds a crystal above my tummy, which does nothing. She sets the crystal down and goes to work, tapping, poking, and rubbing my tired frame. I feel things rush through my body at different angles. She grabs my right foot and holds my right hand, and I can feel a buzz run through me in a circle. She holds my left foot and left hand and I feel the same sensation.

When the hour is over, I feel light as a feather. SueEllen holds her crystal over my belly again, and it swirls in a pleasing circle. "That's much better," she says.

She walks me to my car and gives me a hug. "You're amazing," she yells to me as I pull out of her driveway.

One day I realize I've grown tired of the weirdness, and the darker aspects of this place. There's a cult crackdown in town. The guy with scissors is arrested for child sex trafficking, and the guy who can make your pancreas breathe oxygen is arrested for multiple counts of child sex abuse. The Goddess Temple ladies are merely arrested for *adult* prostitution, so really, they're the rockstars of the cult folk in town.

I've watched people be preyed upon for years. It begins in empowerment and transcendence, and ends in bankruptcy and kids getting hurt, because anyone who asks you to empty yourself to take them into you, or to rid yourself of you so that you can think like them, or to join any kind of hive mind thought system that promises to take you up a notch, or rid you of pain, or make you the you that you always dreamed you could be is completely and utterly full to the brim with dog shit and should be avoided like the plague.

Then a group of well-intentioned people follow a bullshit guru into a sweat lodge out by the Fraudem tent, but it isn't a real sweat lodge. It's a poorly ventilated plastic tent, and they're under no medical supervision there. By the time the group figures out they're in trouble, three of them are already dead, and it's SueEllen—who happens to be hiking by at time—who tries to revive them with CPR.

There comes a night I walk into a house party, set my host gift—a bottle of wine—on a table, and notice a silly-looking contraption sitting in the middle of it. "Is that an E-meter" I ask and chuckle. "Yes, it is," says the host, ushering me toward a bookshelf exclusively stocked with L. Ron Hubbard texts. *Okay. We are leaving now,* I think to myself.

I decide that Arizona has been *just* the place I needed in my life to figure my shit out and get whole—and for that, I will always be thankful—but the time has come to move on to the next phase of my life, and that phase won't be happening here.

THE FULL MOON

ARIZONA

It's a beautiful spring night in Arizona. I'm washing my RV in the dark to get it ready to sell, which is admittedly not the time to be doing such things. I plan to move to Austin, Texas, when I can get it sold.

It's a full moon tonight, and much brighter than usual. SueEllen says that anything is possible when the moon is full.

I haven't seen my parents in several years. They write me emails every so often and when I reply in angry but honest ways, they don't respond. My father asks to come see me, and I say "I don't think so." I want to type something edgier, something like "No fucking way, chief," and maybe sign it "-Your Asshole Daughter" but I don't really want to hurt his feelings, either.

I never wanted to hurt him. I just wanted him to not be so goddamn *mean*.

Mom sends presents every Christmas with greeting cards. The cards say how much she loves me, and I feel terrible when I read them. I know these sentiments are true, and I also know my mother has no clue what love really is, and also thinks control is the same as love, and that none of this is her fault.

But toward the end of my stay in Arizona, my anger melts a little. I genuinely miss my parents and sister, and I begin to think about the good times we had together, the fun trips we took, and how there were times we forgot our internal struggles and we were a genuinely warm family and looked out for each other.

But I feel badly that I've put them out of my life, and I don't know how I can reach out to them again.

As it turns out, on this mild spring night—while spraying the green gunk from the hood of my RV—I will not have to do much to reach out, because my father is in my driveway on the back of a motorcycle.

He takes his helmet off and smiles, and his Irish eyes turn to half moons.

I want to be angry. I really do. I want to tell him to go back to New York.

But I've *never* been so happy to see anyone in my lifetime.

• • •

My father waves the bartender over and orders us another round of beers.

He wasn't around much, did I notice? *Yeah, I did*.

Poor Mom had problems, did I know? *Yep*.

I was an extremely sensitive child, was I aware of that? *Oh, yes. Oh, yes I was.*

I listen and I try to understand. He reveals these *obvious* things to me as if I didn't *bring them right to him* a hundred times when I was young, and he does it with such sincerity and emotion in his voice, I know he honestly believes this is the first time I have considered them.

I always wondered if he saw me when I was little, and the answer is no. He did not; not at all.

To me, he was a ghost. To him, I was a growler.

We missed each other. Maybe the next life?

Maybe.

Until then, I'll take him in from afar, like some wild animal. Maybe that's enough, or if it's not enough, perhaps it just *is*. Maybe it is all there will ever be.

Murph never liked Granger. No matter how many times I brought her to Granger's office, she always sneered at her from the other side of the picture window with a stank snout, because she knew Granger was a little rotten on the inside.

But Murph *adores* my father.

We all get a wave. We do. Every one of us inherits a wave; it's just a part of being human.

Dad never tells me what's in his wave. He doesn't need to for me to know that his wave is ten times taller than mine, and that it is blacker and more formidable than anything I could imagine.

My mother's isn't any less horrible.

We all get a wave, and it crashes down. We hold it back as best we can for the sake of our kids, but some of it gets through. Their wave leaked onto me and it tore me up a little, but the majority they held it back. They tried.

Some kids are lucky, and they are raised in a cocoon of unconditional parental love. They grow a self there as all kids ought to—peaceably and without conflict.

Other kids are forged on the anvil of their parents.

If you're an anvil kid, it takes a bit of hard work to get to where the lucky kids float to in life.

But never curse that anvil. That anvil is a blessing, because it will make you one tough motherfucker.

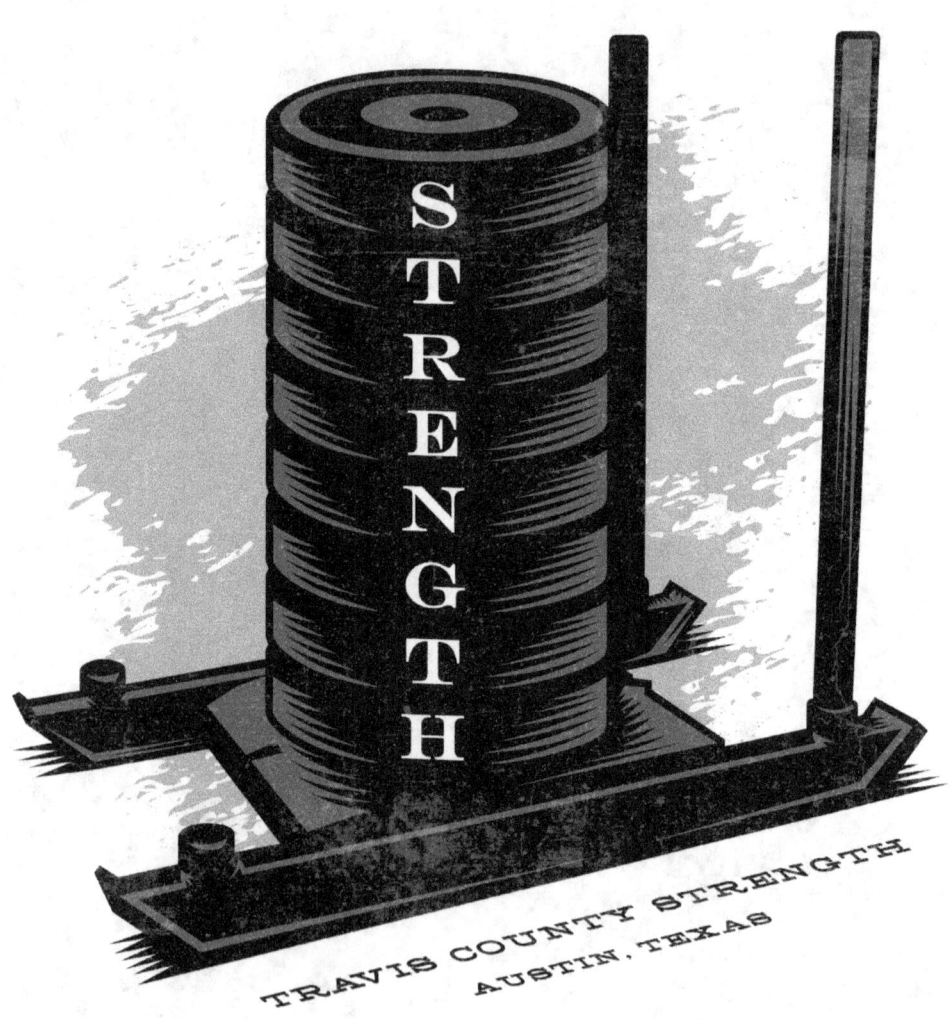

ow much weight is that?

I try to count the plates in my head. I am still piss-poor at math.

It's a hot summer day and the blacktop is viscous. It creates a sort of stickiness between it and the feet of the sled, making it harder to push, which makes this an unlikely day for personal records.

Mary J. Blige is playing through the speakers. My classmates pull plates from stacks and slide them onto the center pole of their sleds before grabbing the handles, dropping a level and leaning in.

They're mothers and entrepreneurs. They're students and artists. They're firefighters and engineers. They're *monsters*. Every one of them is strong, and I am stronger in knowing them. I am blessed to call them my friends.

My coach, Jen, comes to help. She knows I can't do math. She tells me the weight, and it seems daunting. It is dinosaur or semi truck weight. Its a bus. She slaps me on the ass and says, "Do it."

I walk it across the parking lot, turn it around and walk it back. My lungs are on fire. I may shit my pants.

I can hear my compadres cheering as I cross. "Yes!" they say.

I hop over to where Murph is leashed in a corner. I grab her cheeks and kiss the divot in her forehead between her eyebrows. She chirps a little, as if to say "Oh, mom." Her snout is grayed at the end, now, as she's become a beautiful old lady dog—one who definitely still likes food.

I walk over to the plate rack and pull more weight. My philosophy: *clearly, it must be done.*

And if it cannot be done, that's okay too. So long as it is tried.

There's a cheering sound from inside the gym, as one of my monster friends drives out of a squat. The barbell is so heavy, it is bending over her back.

I slide the plate onto my stack and stand before my sled, taking a beat to breathe and to get my shit together.

I let go of a lot, here at this gym. I let go of fear and doubt. I let go of my anger toward others and left old pain in the form of stale sweat on the mats. I flipped tires and tossed kegs like I tossed bad people from my life, and I carried yokes and stones and logs and sandbags wherever I decided they would go, because I chose to put them there of my own volition.

My choice. *Mine.*

Some days I hold the weight of my nineteen-year-old body over my head and I wonder how I could have thought that disappearing from the world like that was the best course of action.

No, *everything* I want to do must be done, and I must be strong enough to do it.

I push the sled across the parking lot, and then I turn it around and push it back.

I stand upright, breathless; my legs burn. I hear cheering.

I never get stomachaches anymore.

that strange and wonderful fullness

Murph is nine when I move to Austin. She develops severe epilepsy. She'll be right as rain for three weeks and then suddenly collapse, lose her urine, and bang her head into the floor as seizures come in waves, again and again. I squirt liquid Valium into her ass with a plastic syringe to sedate her, and hold her tail down to keep the Valium in.

I put a tennis ball in her mouth so she doesn't bite through her tongue, and sometimes I am too late and her mouth fills with blood. I hold her down and whisper anything comforting that I can think to say. "It's okay, baby. You're okay. Mommy is here. You're okay."

But there isn't *anything* okay about it.

Her squeals of fear feel like knives in my heart, and if I could, I'd give her epilepsy to myself instead, so that she'd never have a seizure again.

Sometimes I can't stop the seizures with the Valium, and she has to go to the emergency vet for the night. These stays and her meds are the biggest expenditure in my life, but I'd rather be homeless than live without Murph, and even on heavy doses of meds, Murph is still full of joy and wanton food lust.

When Murph grows a tumor at ten, it grows in the way of Murph, which is to say it grows vigorously, and it takes over her whole side. I have it surgically removed, but in time it grows back, and her vet tells me that there is nothing more I can do to keep her in my life.

She begins to fade away.

When I sense we only have one more night, I cook her a steak for dinner. She wolfs it down whole, her big meatball eyes aglow. By midnight, she's curled up in the corner of the kitchen in pain. I lie there with her all night, to keep her company. I stroke her and say, "It's okay," but much like the epilepsy, there is absolutely *nothing* okay about this.

So I carry her to the vet's office. I thank her for being my dog, and I tell her how much I love her, how I could not have asked for a better dog to spend my life with. She eats one last biscuit, and then the vet hits the plunger. My

Heeler girl is gone forever.

I've long since identified that strange and wonderful fullness I felt when Murph became my dog: it was my very first taste of unconditional love.

When I found Murph, I felt loved for the first time in my life.

She healed me in a deep, unreachable place that no human being could have ever gotten to, and when she's gone, I fear I'll never have a love like that again.

BEAUTIFULLY BORING

2018

AUSTIN, TEXAS

It's a cold morning, a rare and beautiful thing in Texas. There's a breeze blowing through the window, fluttering the curtains. My dog, Ellie, is curled up at my side, waiting patiently—and very unlike Murph—for me to wake up when I feel like doing so. She has excellent manners. She sees me stir a little and rolls onto her back in the crook of my arm like a baby. I scratch her belly and smile as her tail thumps into the bedding. She's a Heeler girl, too, a red one this time. I always try to adopt a Heeler girl.

I yawn and flip the covers off my legs. My joints crack out a little singsong of, "We're in our forties!"

My husband, TJ, is in the living room on the sofa, his laptop perched on his belly. "Hi, baby," I whisper, leaning down to kiss him on the forehead. Ellie growls a little out of jealousy. He's researching fun things to do today—an escape room we haven't tried yet.

"Cool!" I say. "Let's do it."

I found my husband on Tinder, of all places, and when we met, I looked into his big meatball eyes and knew he was my guy. After a lifetime of kissing the worst frogs, it was so easy to say "I do." As SueEllen would say: *the universe provides.*

I let Ellie out to pee and leave the door ajar. A pleasant breeze blows through the living room.

I sit down on the sofa with my husband's feet in my lap, drinking my morning coffee and reading news stories. My mother texts me from an Upstate New York Sam's Club. There's a great sale on stretch pants, $9.99 a pair. She wants to know how many I want and what color they should be. I tell her she has to stop buying me things; I have enough stuff.

I decide to call her because I want to hear her voice. She doesn't pick up the phone because she's practically deaf. She'll call me later.

I hear soft footsteps on the stairs, and then my son, Kylar, pads into the living room. He's barefoot in his PJs, and he rubs his eyes with his fists to wake them up. Ellie trots over to him and rears onto her back legs. She presses her face into his tummy and wraps her paws around him in a hug. He scratches her ears and tells her she's a good dog.

"Hi bud!" I say. I give him a hug and kiss his cheek. I ask him how he slept and if he had any cool dreams.

"I don't remember," he says. I love that his dreams are so uncomplicated.

I ask if he wants juice. "Yes, please," he says. I go to the kitchen to pour some, and hear my husband protest from the couch. "He can get his own damn juice."

Ellie bolts to the stairs, down which comes my eldest son, Gage. I wrap him in my arms and kiss the side of his head. Ellie circles us twice, her collar and tags jingling like a bell.

My boys were nine and twelve when I first met them. We went to a dog park and they threw sticks in a lake for Murph to fetch. We played a few rounds of mini-golf and I kept the scorecard, which it turns out we didn't need, because my

Gage is math genius and kept score in his head. Kylar didn't want anyone to record his score, so I drew him a new picture of his choosing for every hole.

Gage would get a three, TJ would get a four, Erin would get a five, and Kylar would get a turtle, a tank or a rocket.

We get dressed and eat breakfast at a diner, and I sneak Ellie bits of omelet when my husband isn't looking. Then we solve puzzles at the escape room and celebrate our great success with ice cream.

Later we play Risk: the Game of World Domination at the dining room table. Gage takes Australia and Asia and Kylar takes the Americas. TJ takes Africa, and I set up my men in Europe and almost immediately realize that I have made a mistake, because Europe can be attacked from all sides. Kylar wipes out my husband's territories in Africa, and Gage plays little border games with me in China. Hours later, it is clear the only gambit left for either of my boys is an attack on Europe, and neither one of them will do it because they don't want to hurt my feelings. Of course, I could never attack either of them, so the rounds pass and we get bored and give up.

We order pizza and watch an action movie in the living room under blankets. Ellie tries to insert herself into the two inches of space between TJ and me, and gets scolded and banished to her dog bed in the corner of the living room. She chews a little on one of her rawhides, stopping every so often to glare.

The boys get tired and I hug and kiss them goodnight. I love you, I tell them. "Love you too," they say. I never thought I could love anyone as much as I loved Murph, and I certainly never thought I'd love anyone more.

I kiss my husband on the cheek and go to bed, setting my alarm for the morning. I can hear my washing machine sing a little "I am done" song. I hear my husband sneak chocolate cookies from the kitchen when he thinks I am asleep. I worry a little about the things adults worry about, tomorrow's calls with clients and making sure I have time to pick up groceries for the week.

For decades I had spent my nights worrying and obsessing over myself, sorting through any little bit of flotsam I could find floating around in the big big hole that should have been a me, trying to make sense of how I felt. These days I don't think about myself all that much; I simply live. My biggest concern is the happiness of my family, and though no family is perfect—we are far from it, and have all the usual problems families have—I find it so pleasant being a "we."

Often, the weird, beautifully boring life I have now doesn't seem real to me. I can remember, many years ago, thinking of such lives—so peaceful and so void of drama—and believing with a terrible sense of certainty that they could never happen to me because I was cursed and I was bad. No one would ever want someone so broken. I was not deserving of love. Now, my life is full of it.

TJ and I got married in Costa Rica. My father walked me down the aisle in a silk shirt and snappy straw hat. He was beaming with pride like the day I walked into the kitchen and found him holding my scholarship letter.

Before the wedding, he sent my husband a stuffed goat, as a

sort of dowry joke that—not unlike my father's other comedic gems—sank like a stone. The note attached read, "Once you cash this, you can't give her back."

I actually laughed a little as I read it, and it seemed silly if it seemed like anything at all.

Oh dad.

This is the lovely thing about having self esteem. You could *suggest* I was or am a burden, but I know I am *not*. In fact, I know that I never was. Feel free to disagree with me; I am still going to love you.

And I will never forget what I'm worth.

Life is without meaning.
You bring the meaning to it.
The meaning of life is whatever
you ascribe it to be.

—Joseph Campbell

When I look back on my time with Granger, it is with great fondness.

I can't argue she's an ethical therapist, and I'm not going to make excuses for her behavior. I'll only say that we all get a wave.

I appreciate Granger's intelligence, how she knew exactly what stories to tell me, and how those stories opened me up to change, and ultimately altered the course of my path in life, which is precisely what I went to therapy looking to find.

Long ago on that cold night I lay drunk on my grandmother's couch—Mark's body not yet cold in the ground—I didn't have the foggiest of ideas about why I needed to write down my new thoughts in that notebook. I only knew that I felt powerful when I did it. Later on, I called that power "the writing process" but that was probably a misnomer. It wasn't writing that made me feel powerful; it was finally *having control over my own story*.

I don't think I had ever really been suicidal. I simply wanted my life to be mine.

It hurt to be cast as the villain in a story that wasn't mine. I didn't want to wear the sinister mustache and be everyone's problem, and subsequently the reason they all came back together again—and no one should have forced me to do it.

Taking out that notebook and pen, and writing down my thoughts was the beginning of a total rewrite of my life. It was a decision to side with myself.

I had a blog a long time ago, and it helped a lot of people. I put off publishing a book for many years, decades even. Writing is a personal endeavor for me—and when I do it, I do it for myself—and I never wanted to share personal details about my parents' struggles with the world, because I love my parents and I believe they did their best for me. Hell, I've never wanted them to feel anything but wanted and appreciated, but we've already established that I can't reach back into the fifties and change what happened there.

Sometimes I think about my past and shudder. I drank myself into a CAT scan, and went head first down a stone stairwell. I bounced off cars into intersections, turned my knees into hamburger and spent god knows how many hours—weeks, months maybe—shoving pens and toothbrushes into my gullet to wretch food back out of my belly into buckets and bags and toilets, hanging upside down with blood pooling in my face, and snot and spit running down my forearm. My heart beating so fast it could break.

That's not even the worst of it. The enemy in my head with the fresh insult every sixth second, with the berating and mocking and humiliating, and the drowning out of all other things—all the good things I should have had—the pushing away of every living soul on this earth, because I didn't deserve to feel affection, or love, or joy, or anything but the despair of loneliness? That was the worst.

I hung out with a rapist. I *had* to know he was a rapist.

I stole the rapist's drugs and I took them so I didn't have to be me any more, and of course they could have been baby aspirins, but they were probably hard drugs, and it may seem silly to say, but I believe if it hadn't been for the music, I wouldn't be here to write this.

And what is music, anyway?

Stories. It's just stories.

※

I have one last story to tell. It's about a little devil who came to my door two years ago.

It was a drizzly Halloween night. We didn't bother to light the pumpkins, and my husband set a little awning up over the front door to keep the kids dry when they came for candy.

It was still early in the night when the doorbell rang, and I opened it to see a little girl in a devil costume. She had short black hair and a hole in her mouth where one or two teeth had recently been. She was about six years old, and quite shy. She looked up at me, smiled, and held out a black pillowcase full of little boxes of sweets and various chocolate bars.

"Say 'Trick or treat,'" said Mom from a few feet away under a golf umbrella with what must have been Dad.

"Twick or tweat," she said. It was fucking adorable.

I tried to be an adult, I swear. I didn't *want* to project.

I tried to consider that this sweet little thing may actually think a devil is a neat thing to be for Halloween, or that should could have gone to the store looking for a princess costume, spied this red sparkly number she had on now, and honestly wanted to wear it for Halloween. That's pretty punk rock, if you think about it.

I tried to consider that Mom and Dad had nothing to do with her choice, and that they were emotionally self aware enough to not hold this child accountable for how they might feel about themselves. I swear I tried to think this while rooting through the pile of treats in my wooden salad bowl to find the best stuff, the peanut butter cups, and the Crunch candy bars, and one or two Skittles.

But I *failed*. I was too frightened.

I dumped the candy into her bag, and I called her parents a variety of unsavory names under my breath as they walked her back down my driveway and into the night.

After that I paced around my house, heated and perturbed. I couldn't stop thinking about her sweet little face in that devil costume.

Would this little girl grow to hate herself? Would she think she deserved love? Would she be one of those kids I see so often these days, who measures her self worth by social media likes, and doesn't have a clue that there's a difference between seeming like something and being it? Would she hurt herself and stand in her own way? God forbid she do to herself what I did to me.

I realized that it wasn't enough to write my story. I had to tell it too.

I can't start the acknowledgments with anyone but Tucker Max, whose unfailing encouragement made this project possible. Thank you for reading hundreds of pages full of raw, abstract feelings, and thank you for your relentlessly honest notes about them. Thank you for the endless kicks to the ass, and for being the kind of friend who won't allow you to betray yourself.

Thank you to my amazing husband, TJ, and to my kick ass sons, Gage and Kylar who make every day a Saturday. My life would mean nothing without you.

Thanks to my incredible friend Charlie Hoehn, who was always there when I needed a sounding board, glass of champagne, or ride on a scooter.

Thank you to JT McCormick for being the purest embodiment of what the word "leader" means.

Thank you to my second family, the Tribe at Scribe media, for your boundless and humbling love and support, and special thanks to Amanda Ibey, Harlan Clifford, Natalie Aboudaoud, Meghan McCracken, and April Kelly.

Sincere thanks to my mother-in-law, Carol Mahoney; sisters-in-law Wendy Hoverson and Terry Gullixson; the whole Mahoney Clan; Phyllis Nelson, James K. Nelson II, one of the world's most accomplished story tellers; and Sheila, Amanda, and Matt Nelson. Thanks as well to the whole Tyler clan.

Thanks to the primal force of nature that is SueEllen Trumbour-Cheney.

Thanks to Lindsay Oram, Krissie Weimer, Nicole Prinzi, Leah Gerstel, Jennie Terreberry, Jen Shaw, Jodi Swanson, Max Wong, Ann Maynard, Bob Doverspike, Swami Grace Dorman, Dr. Cindy Peterson, Deborah Oram and to the many kind souls who wrote in support of the Bunny Blog. Your encouragement and support during my rougher times warmed my heart.

Thanks to my fur babies, Ellie and Sadie.

And finally, thanks to my sweet, sweet Murph angel. I'd give anything to pull just one more length of mint-flavored dental floss out of your ass.

About The Author

I think you've probably heard enough about me.

www.ingramcontent.com/pod-product-compliance
Lightning Source LLC
Chambersburg PA
CBHW070046080526
44586CB00013B/935